NATIVE PLANTS OF AOTEAROA

NATIVE PLANTS OF AOTEAROA

Carlos Lehnebach
Heidi Meudt

CONTENTS

Introduction	7
About this book	12
The plants	15
Glossary	118
References	122
Image credits	126
Acknowledgements	127
Index of species	128
About the authors	131

INTRODUCTION

Aotearoa New Zealand is an archipelago with extremely diverse landscapes and habitats. It includes Te Ika-a-Māui North Island, Te Waipounamu South Island and Rakiura Stewart Island, and a number of outlying islands such as Manawatāwhi Three Kings Islands, Rangitāhua Kermadec Islands, Rēkohu Chatham Islands and a few subantarctic islands. Overall, Aotearoa covers an area of around 265,000 sq km and recent estimates suggest that it has almost 2400 native species of vascular plants (i.e. ferns, conifers and flowering plants). Nearly 80 percent of these plants are endemic, meaning they are found nowhere else.

Daisies, grasses and sedges are the three plant families with the greatest number of species in the country – the daisy family alone comprises almost 600 species. Ironically, the number of introduced plant species (about 2900) is higher than the number of natives. However, the number of known native species is still growing, with botanists estimating that almost 300 potential new species are waiting to be studied and formally described.

There is something of a myth that plant species in Aotearoa are dull. At first glance that might appear to be the case, but look closer. Aotearoa has been separated from other land masses for more than 80 million years. Isolation, and the fortuitous arrival of species from nearby areas, have resulted in the evolution of unique plants with curious adaptations to their environment and the local fauna. The native flora of Aotearoa is distinguished in several ways:

- Many of our plants, such as pōānanga (Forster's clematis, *Clematis forsteri*; page 51), have simple bowl-shaped flowers. This makes their nectar easily accessible to whatever insect visits them and is an adaptation to generalist pollinators. The flower shape matches the preferences of flies, the most abundant and common pollinators in Aotearoa, which include more than 2000 species. Birds are common pollinators, too, whereas butterflies and bees are not well represented in the fauna of Aotearoa.

- The flowers of alpine plants, including pekapeka (mountain daisy, *Celmisia gracilenta*; page 25), are mostly white. This feature is especially obvious when comparing the flowers of native species with relatives in the northern hemisphere, such as forget-me-nots (e.g. *Myosotis forsteri*; page 37) and gentians, which are mostly blue in Europe. Again, this is an adaptation to local pollinators.

- Deciduous trees, such as kōtukutuku (tree fuchsia, *Fuchsia excorticata*; page 77), are uncommon due to the relatively mild winters in Aotearoa, which means that evergreen trees – including rimu (*Dacrydium cupressinum*; page 69), tawa (*Beilschmiedia tawa*; page 61) and many others – abound.

- Aotearoa has a number of dioecious species, where male and female flowers are borne on separate individuals. They include kōhia (New Zealand passionflower, *Passiflora tetrandra*; page 53), makomako (wineberry, *Aristotelia serrata*; page 57) and four other species described in this book. This strategy promotes cross-pollination between genetically distinct plants and consequently increases genetic diversity.

- Some woody plants, such as kāmahi (*Pterophylla racemosa*; page 103), have different juvenile and adult forms. These 'shapeshifting' species can change the size, shape and lobing of their leaf margins over the course of their life, a feature that makes identification difficult.

- There is an abundance of divaricating shrubs. These are plants with small leaves on tough, wiry stems that have a tight, dense, interlocking branching pattern. This growth form is believed to have evolved as a defence against browsing by moa.

- The megaherbs of the subantarctic islands have unique adaptations. Unlike plants on the mainland, their leaves are very large, thick and hairy, and their flowers deep shades of pink, yellow and purple. These adaptations are believed to help them harvest heat whenever the sun is shining, a rare event at such latitudes. The heat they trap then attracts insects, which in turn pollinate the flowers.

The long-term survival of our unique flora is, however, endangered by a number of threats. These include habitat destruction; the consumption of flowers, seedlings and leaves by introduced animals (browsing); weed invasion; pathogens; and the disruption of beneficial interactions between plants and their pollinators or seed dispersers following the introduction of predators. Of these threats, habitat destruction and browsing are likely the most serious. For instance, in the past one hundred years almost 90 percent of wetlands in Aotearoa have been drained for urban or rural development. This means that habitats of many wetland specialists, such as orchids and insectivorous plants, have disappeared. Browsing by introduced animals on flowers, seedlings and leaves on the other hand, has caused considerable damage to the reproduction and regeneration of many plant and tree species. The introduction of possums from Australia in the 1850s, for instance, has been linked with the extinction of the Adams mistletoe (*Trilepidea adamsii*), last seen in 1954.

Currently, almost half of our vascular flora is considered to be of conservation concern, and is listed as Threatened or At Risk in the New Zealand Threat Classification System. The NZTCS assesses the conservation status of all indigenous vascular plants against four main categories (Extinct, Threatened, At Risk, Not Threatened). Assessments are based on population size, number of mature individuals and area of occupancy, and are reviewed every five years. This work helps the Department of Conservation (DOC) to manage threatened species, allocate resources and prioritise conservation efforts. Unfortunately, listing a species under these threat categories does not necessarily confer legal protection. Unlike other countries, New Zealand law does not protect threatened plants unless they are found on conservation land (national parks, reserves and conservation areas).

BOTANICAL COLLECTIONS AT TE PAPA

With almost 300,000 dried pressed plant specimens (and counting!), the botany collection at The Museum of New Zealand Te Papa Tongarewa is one of the largest collections at the museum. Its origin goes back to 1865, when the Colonial Museum (Te Papa's predecessor) was founded. Back then, there was great interest among European scientists for recording the plants and natural resources found in the new colonies. These activities involved the exploration of the diverse landscapes of Aotearoa and, inevitably, the documentation of many plant species new to the Western world. James Hector, the first director of the Colonial Museum, decided that a reference collection was indispensable to support the research of local botanists and instigated the creation of the herbarium. Today, the herbarium stores dried, pressed specimens of marine algae, lichens, liverworts, mosses, ferns, conifers and flowering plants collected in Aotearoa and around the world.

More than 150 years later, this collection continues to grow. Current efforts aim to document introduced species, record the plant diversity from remote areas of Aotearoa and describe the diversity within poorly studied plant groups. Just like those early botanists, our botany curators are also tasked with taxonomic research to document the country's biodiversity. In the past decade, they have described and named more than twenty plant species and conducted numerous collection trips to coastal and alpine areas and offshore islands within Aotearoa, as well as to islands in the Pacific region.

Surprisingly, modern plant-collecting techniques have not changed much from those used by naturalists Joseph Banks and Daniel Solander when they first landed in Aotearoa more than 250 years ago with Captain James Cook. Basically, fresh plants are collected, labelled, placed in between paper and cardboard, and then tightly pressed. Technological advances mean that botanists can now use a large dryer to speed up the drying process, and ultra-cold freezers have replaced chemicals to kill insects that might feed on and damage the specimens later. Specimens are then databased, imaged, stored in special cabinets in temperature- and humidity-controlled vaults, and made available via Collections Online (collections.tepapa.govt.nz). Specialised microscopes and a fully equipped DNA lab at the museum allow morphological and genetic study of these plants, respectively.

Curators are entrusted with the care and preservation of Te Papa's collections. Making them accessible and sharing their stories with the public is an important aspect of their role. In fact, the botanical collections and their stories reach far beyond the museum's walls. For instance, the collections underpin the research of postgraduate students, scientists and historians around Aotearoa and overseas, and inspire the work of artists and designers. For curators, expanding and caring for these collections also means working in collaboration with scientists from national and international universities, Crown research institutes such as Manaaki Whenua – Landcare Research, DOC, botanic gardens, iwi, private landowners, and community groups interested in the flora of Aotearoa and its conservation, including botanical societies, the New Zealand Native Orchid Group and iNaturalist. These collections-based collaborations see Te Papa curators going on joint field trips with local iwi representatives to collect plant specimens on their land, loaning specimens to researchers at other herbaria worldwide, and giving virtual and in-person behind-the-scenes herbarium tours to schools and other interested groups.

As well as sharing its botanical collections for research purposes, the museum also tells the stories of the specimens through exhibitions and books. A great place to start learning about the plants in this book, including more details on their unique adaptations, is the Endemic Wall in Te Papa's Te Taiao | Nature exhibition. Or on a visit to the museum, you could see how many of the plants you can spot growing just outside its walls in Bush City, Te Papa's only living exhibition – use the descriptions and illustrations in this book to help you.

Observing and learning about our native plants, and increasing awareness about them by teaching others, are important aspects of te kaitiakitanga o te taiao – environmental stewardship. Kaitiakitanga is everyone's responsibility, including specialist curators, day walkers, children, grandparents, community groups, iwi, companies, governments and museums. Our collections form the heart of the museum's kaitiakitanga, which extends into the community as well. Each of us has a duty to be a kaitiaki or guardian of our native flora, which includes observing plants, learning about them and sharing our knowledge, and doing our bit to protect them and their habitats. You might join a local botanical society, start backyard trapping with a local Predator Free New Zealand group, share your observations of plants on the iNaturalist website, or grow native plants in your garden. The more we know about our native plants – including their names, whakapapa or origins, features, adaptations, significance and stories – the better we will value our natural world and understand our place in it.

Carlos Lehnebach, Heidi Meudt

ABOUT THIS BOOK

This book provides useful descriptions alongside simple yet beautiful historical illustrations. Anyone will be able to find and observe some of these plants, appreciate their beauty and quirks, learn their stories, and discuss them with friends and whānau.

The fifty plant species are listed by growth form, with ferns first, followed by herbs, vines and, finally, shrubs and trees. Within each group, species are ordered alphabetically by scientific name. An index of species names is provided at the back.

The illustrations are based on sketches by Sydney Parkinson, who was the artist on board HMS *Endeavour* during the 1768–71 expedition led by Captain James Cook. Parkinson's field drawings were made from fresh plant specimens collected in the southern hemisphere by botanists Joseph Banks and Daniel Solander. Sadly, Parkinson died on the return voyage, having contracted malaria in Java. After the voyage, Banks employed five artists to complete Parkinson's sketches, and eighteen engravers to create exquisite copperplate line engravings from these drawings. These plates are now held by the National History Museum in London. There have been just two occasions on which prints have been made from these plates. The first, in the late nineteenth century, as sets of black and white proof prints; and the second, in the 1980s, when an elaborate enterprise was undertaken to produce limited edition sets of 743 colour prints. These are collectively called *Banks' Florilegium*.

Te Papa holds a set of the black and white engravings, gifted to the Colonial Museum in the 1890s. These were originally intended to illustrate Thomas Kirk's *The Students' Flora of New Zealand and the Outlying Islands* (1899), the first book about the flora of Aotearoa by a resident botanist. Unfortunately, Kirk died before the book was published and the prints were not included. It seems appropriate, then, that over one hundred years later they are published here with the same desire to make the plants of Aotearoa better understood and appreciated by the amateur botanist. These prints are the perfect illustrations for *Native Plants of Aotearoa* owing to their beauty, scientific accuracy, history and precise black-on-white reproduction. The biggest challenge for the authors was having to choose a selection of the 185 prints!

Some plants were selected because they were of most interest to the curators, including some that are part of their own research programmes (forget-me-nots, plantains and orchids). Other plants were chosen because they had an interesting story to tell, or because of the striking beauty of their illustrations. Finally, although this guide is not comprehensive, the aim was to make it practical by choosing plants that can be commonly encountered throughout Aotearoa.

The descriptions are written in an accessible manner, reducing the number of scientific terms and jargon. However, a glossary is included at the end of the book for those technical terms that simply could not be avoided.

THE PLANTS

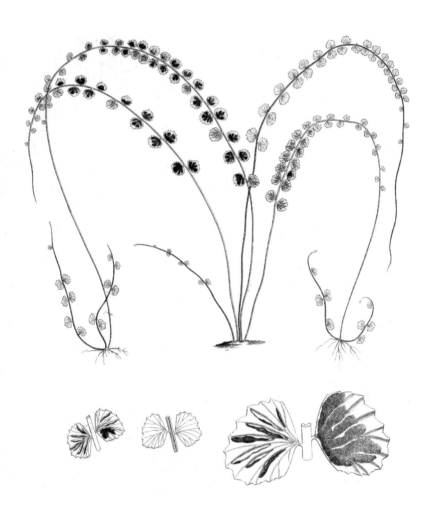

BUTTERFLY FERN

Asplenium flabellifolium

The three common names of this fern – butterfly, necklace and walking fern – highlight its unique form. Butterfly fern refers to the fan-like shape of its pinnae (the species name *flabellifolium* means 'fan-shaped leaves'), which resemble multiple butterflies hovering along the rachis, or stem. The curved fronds also resemble the beads of a long, curved necklace. Finally, the fronds give rise to new plants at the tips of the rachis, revealing the secret to the slow march of the walking fern.

Habitat and distribution: Dry rocky habitats in forest, shrubland and grassland of lowland and montane areas throughout Te Ika-a-Māui North Island and Te Waipounamu South Island. Also native to Australia.

Description: This fern has short, erect, scaly rhizomes. Its looping fronds are narrowly linear, up to 50cm long, with a red-brown rachis. The middle third of the rachis bears the leafy portion of the frond, which is up to 30cm long and is divided into 4–25 pairs of pinnae. The pinnae are light green, flaccid, often prostrate, up to 2mm long and 2mm wide, and fan-shaped with rounded tips and toothed margins. The rachis extends up to 20cm beyond the pinnae and may be rooting at the tip. The spore-producing sori are located along the veins and away from the pinna margins.

PIRIPIRI
BIDIBID

Acaena anserinifolia

One of the most notable aspects of piripiri is the barb-tipped spines on the fruit. These spines allow the fruits of this endemic species to attach to passing animals, which then disperse these to new sites. In other parts of the world mammals are usually responsible for carrying such spiny seeds, but in Aotearoa New Zealand flightless birds with loose feathers, such as kiwi or weka, are the unwitting couriers.

Habitat and distribution: Herbfields, grassland, shrubland and open habitats of lowland, montane or subalpine areas. Common throughout Te Ika-a-Māui North Island, Te Waipounamu South Island, Rakiura Stewart Island, Rēkohu Chatham Islands and Motu Maha Auckland Islands.

Description: A hairy perennial herb with a creeping stolon up to 1m long, from which protrude ascending to erect stems up to 15cm long. The oblong leaves are up to 8cm long and have 9–13 serrated leaflets, as well as a toothed stipule at the base. The upper surface of the leaf is dull to brownish green, whereas the lower surface is pale green. The peduncles can be up to 12cm long, and are capped with an inflorescence that is a spiny spherical head, 1–2cm in diameter, when flowering or fruiting. The head comprises dozens of tiny flowers, each with four reddish sepals, two stamens with white anthers and one white feathery style. Each small flower develops into a small cone-shaped fruit about 3mm long, which is crowned with four brown barbed spines that are each about 2–3 times as long as the fruit itself.

TARAMEA
SPEARGRASS

Aciphylla squarrosa

Despite the species' fiercely pointed leaves, browsing of taramea by introduced mammals has caused extensive damage to many populations of this plant across Aotearoa. The extent of damage is such that taramea is now considered a species of conservation concern. Unfortunately, the decline of taramea populations has put another organism under threat of extinction, the Wellington speargrass weevil. This insect has a very specific diet and feeds only on taramea.

Habitat and distribution: Coastal to subalpine zones, on streamsides and wet, shady banks throughout Te Ika-a-Māui North Island and Te Waipounamu South Island.

Description: This robust herb grows up to 1m tall and forms dense clumps. The leaves are spear-like, bluish green, rather soft and highly divided. The leaflets are narrow, about 4mm wide, with a long, sharp tip. Flowering stems are 60–200cm long with many narrow leafy bracts. These bracts have a membranous sheath at the base. The lamina is divided into narrow segments with a stiff pointed tip. Male and female flowers are on different plants. The flowering stem of female plants is longer than that in male plants. The flowers are 2–4mm in diameter with five sepals and five pale yellow petals. The flowers are scented and arranged in umbrella-like inflorescences on stout peduncles 5cm long (female stems) to 6–10cm long (male stems). The fruits are 6–8mm long and have three or four wings.

RENGARENGA
RENGARENGA LILY

Arthropodium cirratum

This plant is easy to cultivate and very popular in gardens. Records from the late 1800s report that plantations of rengarenga were a common sight around kāinga (villages). Māori used the base of their leaves as plasters to treat ulcers, and cooked and ate the fleshy roots. Genetic studies led by Te Papa scientists have confirmed that rengarenga was indeed domesticated by Māori, who transported it around Te Ika-a-Māui North Island and Te Waipounamu South Island. Domestication of this species, however, resulted in the loss of genetic diversity within the cultivated stock.

Habitat and distribution: Coastal to lowland forest, mostly on exposed and rocky areas in Te Ika-a-Māui and Te Waipounamu.

Description: This robust evergreen plant grows up to 1m tall, usually forming extensive colonies. The rhizome is sometimes woody, and 1–2cm thick. The leaves are tightly packed along the rhizome, 30–60cm long and 3–10 cm wide, lance-shaped and slightly fleshy. Inflorescences are borne above the leaves on a stiff multi-branched peduncle. The flowers are held in pedicels 2cm long and joined in groups of 2–3. The flowers are white, 2–4cm in diameter, with six tepals in two whorls. The outer tepals are narrow and of a thicker texture, while the inner tepals are broader, of a thinner texture, and have slightly uneven margins. The stamens are shorter than the tepals. The anthers are very colourful and adorned with a purplish tail at the top, white feathery hairs at the centre and curled golden-yellow ends. The fruits are 8mm long and 6mm wide, with black seeds that are 2mm long and have a bumpy, textured surface.

PEKAPEKA
MOUNTAIN DAISY

Celmisia gracilenta

Mountain daisies are some of the most common alpine plants in Aotearoa, and although their flowering heads are very similar across species, their leaves (shape, size, surface) and growth form are incredibly diverse. Pekapeka may not be the most spectacular species in this genus, but it was the first one collected by the botanists Joseph Banks and Daniel Solander during Captain James Cook's first voyage to Aotearoa in 1769–70. There are more than sixty species of *Celmisia*, most of them found in Aotearoa and a few in Australia.

Habitat and distribution: Lowland to subalpine areas, occupying a wide range of habitats, including subalpine scrub, tussock grassland, herbfields and bogs throughout Te Ika-a-Māui North Island and Te Waipounamu South Island.

Description: This slender, tufted herb has mottled greyish-green leaves that are 10–15cm long and 2–4mm wide. The leaf lamina is linear, with margins rolled almost to the midrib, and is slightly coriaceous, flexible and rather flaccid. The leaf apex is acute and pointed. The upper surface is coated with silvery membrane, while the underside is densely covered with white hairs. Soft white hairs also cover the 25–40cm-long peduncle and its narrow-linear bracts. The peduncle supports the flowers, which are densely packed in a head. The head is 1–2cm in diameter and consists of ray flowers on the outside and disc flowers in the centre. The disc flowers are narrow and up to 1cm long, whereas the ray flowers are up to 2.5cm long. The seeds are about 5mm long and attached to a downy crown of hairs that facilitates seed dispersal by wind.

SUNDEW

Drosera auriculata

This sundew is one of the seven species of the insectivorous plant genus *Drosera* found in Aotearoa. Its leaves are covered in glandular hairs that produce droplets of mucilage, a sweet, sticky substance. This substance attracts insects to the leaf but, once they have landed on it, prevents them from escaping. Enzymes in the mucilage then digest the insect and the nutrients are absorbed through the leaf. This adaptation helps sundews to thrive in soils lacking nitrogen and other nutrients, such as those found in swamps and bogs.

Habitat and distribution: Coastal to montane zones on moist banks and open areas in Te Ika-a-Māui North Island and northern Te Waipounamu South Island.

Description: This carnivorous plant arises every season from a small tuber. The stem is slender, erect or climbing, and up to 30cm or more in length. The basal leaves are arranged in a rosette. The petioles are flat, up to 1cm long, and the leaf lamina is round, 3mm wide and covered in glandular hairs. Stem leaves are arranged in alternating fashion, with a long, thin petiole up to 1.5cm in length. The lamina of stem leaves is shield-shaped and covered in glandular hairs. The flowers are held on a single peduncle up to 10cm long. The sepals are green, elliptic to egg-shaped, with a smooth or jagged margin, and up to 5mm long. The petals are pink, slightly egg-shaped and up to 8mm long. The fruits are tiny capsules, only 2mm across, with minute seeds.

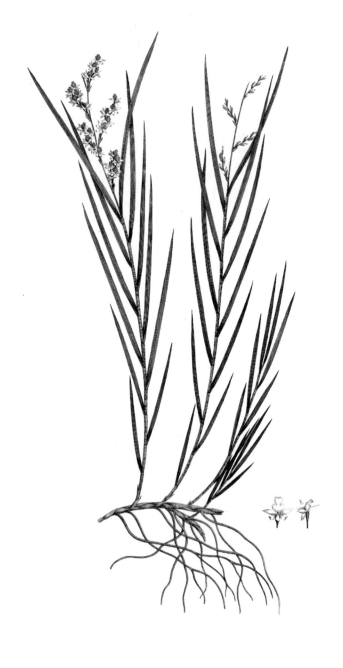

PEKA-A-WAKA
BAMBOO ORCHID

Earina mucronata

Peka-a-waka is one of nine species of epiphytic orchid endemic to Aotearoa. Unlike many tropical orchids, its flowers are simple and the nectar is accessible to any floral visitor. Pollination studies on this and two other epiphytic orchids have recorded at least twenty different insect visitors. This unspecialised pollination is believed to be an adaptation to New Zealand's pollinating fauna, where social bees are lacking and most of the pollination is performed by generalist pollinators such as flies.

Habitat and distribution: Coastal to montane forest, perching on trees, rocks and cliff faces, but also growing in rocky and clay soils in Te Ika-a-Māui North Island, Te Waipounamu South Island, Rakiura Stewart Island and Rēkohu Chatham Islands.

Description: This orchid has spongy, cord-like roots that emerge from a long, scaly, creeping rhizome. There are multiple drooping stems along the rhizome, with old plants forming sizeable clumps. The leaves are 6–10cm long, narrow (4–6mm wide) and grass-like, with a smooth margin and a pointed tip. They are arranged alternately along the stem, each one attached to it by a light brown sheath, resulting in the stem resembling a bamboo cane. The flowers are arranged in clusters of 5–10, and these are grouped together into larger inflorescences. The flowers are small, about 1cm across, and slightly scented. The sepals and petals have smooth margins and are pale yellow or whitish. The labellum is bright orange and divided into three lobes; the mid-lobe is the broadest.

NAU
COOK'S SCURVY GRASS

Lepidium oleraceum

This perennial plant is a member of the cabbage family (Brassicaceae) and has an important place in the history of circumnavigation. During these long voyages, many sailors died of scurvy, a disease caused by the lack of vitamin C. However, this was not the case for the crew of the HMS *Endeavour*. During his first voyage to Aotearoa, Captain James Cook would frequently restock the ship with fresh food and vegetables, and entries in his diary report the crew collecting and eating nau. Little did he know that this plant was rich in vitamin C!

Habitat and distribution: Coastal areas, mostly around seabird nesting sites, on sand and gravel beaches throughout Te Ika-a-Māui North Island, Te Waipounamu South Island and Rakiura Stewart Island. Also on offshore islands such as Rangitāhua Kermadec Islands, Manawatāwhi Three Kings Islands and Moutere Hauriri Bounty Islands.

Description: This plant has a trailing to erect stem more than 50cm tall. The leaves are elliptic to egg-shaped, evenly toothed towards the tip, bright green, fleshy, and 2–10cm long and 1.5–4cm wide. The tiny flowers are 3–4mm across and arranged in inflorescences that appear at the end or on the sides of the branchlets. The inflorescences are 2–9cm long at fruiting. The minute sepals are 1–1.5mm long and 0.5–1mm wide. The petals are white and only slightly larger than the sepals, being 1–2mm long and 1.5–2.5mm wide. The fruits are broadly egg-shaped, usually with a blunt base and pointed tip, 3–4mm long and 2–4mm wide. The seeds are also egg-shaped, brown, and 1–2mm long and 1–1.5mm wide.

MIKOIKOI
NEW ZEALAND IRIS

Libertia grandiflora

This species is one of about a dozen in the genus *Libertia*, which has a Gondwanan distribution, with members also occurring in Australia, New Guinea and southern South America. There are about eight species of *Libertia* in Aotearoa, three of which are of conservation concern, largely owing to habitat destruction. Mikoikoi is currently in cultivation and is often seen in private and street gardens. Bringing threatened species like this into cultivation can help with their conservation by creating a back-up stock in the event that wild populations disappear.

Habitat and distribution: Coastal to montane habitats in Te Ika-a-Māui North Island, usually in forest margins and on streambanks and river terraces.

Description: This plant is about 1m high and consists of leafy fans, closely bunched on short, highly branched rhizomes that are joined by short stolons. The leaves are strappy and thin, 10–140cm long and up to 1cm wide. The flowering stem is long, usually carrying the flowers above the leaves. The flowers are 1–3cm in diameter with two whorls of three tepals each. The external tepals are small and boat-shaped, and are white internally but pigmented on the outer surface. The inner tepals are oblong with a cleft at the tip and white. The anthers are bright yellow. The fruit is a capsule 6–14mm long and 4–8mm wide, shaped like a teardrop, and green but turning black on maturity. The seeds are 1–2mm long and 1–1.5mm wide, rounded or sometimes angular, with a net-like surface that is bright tangerine orange.

PĀNAKENAKE
CREEPING PRATIA

Lobelia angulata

Pānakenake is a delicate creeping endemic plant commonly found throughout the country. Home gardeners appreciate this groundcover for its ability to grow quickly and the beauty of its masses of star-like white flowers in spring. In both the garden and the wild, the distinctive purple berries are attractive to native birds in summer.

Habitat and distribution: Damp, shady habitats, from sea level to subalpine sites throughout Te Ika-a-Māui North Island, Te Waipounamu South Island and Rakiura Stewart Island.

Description: A prostrate herbaceous species that forms mats or patches along the ground. The slender, branched, creeping stems root at the nodes. The leaves are short-petiolate, with leaf blades that are glabrous, round in shape, about 1cm in diameter and toothed along the edges. Each flower is supported by a slender peduncle up to 6cm long. The small calyx is 2–4mm long with linear lobes. The white corollas can be up to 2cm long and are star-shaped and deeply divided, with five pointed oblong lobes. Pānakenake fruits are spherical or oblong red to purple berries about 1cm in diameter and contain many seeds.

FORGET-ME-NOT

Myosotis forsteri

This was one of two native forget-me-nots collected during Captain James Cook's first two voyages to Aotearoa. About fifty such species are now recognised in Aotearoa, many of which are uncommon. It is often necessary to use a microscope to see the minute features that can be used to distinguish the different species from one another!

Habitat and distribution: Damp, shady habitats in the forest understorey. Although widespread throughout Te Ika-a-Māui North Island and Te Waipounamu South Island, its populations are small and sparsely distributed.

Description: This delicate hairy herb has leaves arranged in a rosette at the base. The leaves have long petioles, and round or oval leaf blades that are 1.5–4cm long and 1–3cm wide, being widest near the tip. Arising from the rosette are multiple flowering branches up to 35cm long; these have alternating leaves near the base that are replaced by an inflorescence of small flowers near the tips. The corollas are white, less than 1cm across, with five flaring petals, each with a yellow scale near the corolla tube. The five fused sepals of the calyx have hooked hairs near the base. The fruits are shiny, smooth, brown or black, and up to 1.5mm long. There are up to four of these tiny fruits in each calyx.

BEAD PLANT

Nertera depressa

Nertera is a member of the coffee family (Rubiaceae) and, just as in some species of *Coprosma* in the same family, the leaves produce a very unpleasant smell when crushed. The red–crimson fruits are one of the most striking features of the genus, which is why many *Nertera* species are cultivated as garden or indoor plants. Despite the fruits being only a few millimetres in diameter, *Nertera* was part of the diet of New Zealand's largest bird, the moa, now extinct.

Habitat and distribution: Forest floor and damp banks or permanently wet sites in subalpine settings throughout Te Ika-a-Māui North Island, Te Waipounamu South Island and Rakiura Stewart Island. Also on Rangitāhua Kermadec Islands and Rēkohu Chatham Islands.

Description: This creeping herb forms small to large patches up to 3m in diameter. The four-angled, square stems are mostly hairless, and are faintly to strongly foetid when bruised. The leaves are held on petioles 2–4mm long, or sometimes longer when the plant is growing in shade. Two small triangular stipules, usually rather thick, are found near the base of the petioles. The leaf lamina is egg-shaped or triangular, slightly membranaceous to thick, and 5–8mm long and 3–10mm wide, with thickened margins that are also recurved and sometimes slightly wavy. The flowers are solitary, borne in the leaf axil, sessile and very small. The fruits are fleshy, spherical, bright to dark red, and about 4mm in diameter.

TŪKŌREHU

Plantago raoulii

There are more than 250 species of *Plantago* in the world, eleven of which are native to Aotearoa. Seed features are the easiest way to distinguish tūkōrehu from the other native species: it usually has exactly five seeds per capsule, including one small angular seed found near the top of the fruit, plus four vertical seeds below – two short and two long. You'll need a steady hand and a good hand lens to see them, though – the seeds are only about 1–2mm long! Seeds can be found in summer or early autumn.

Habitat and distribution: Common in open areas of herbfields, grassland, coasts and forests throughout Te Ika-a-Māui North Island, Te Waipounamu South Island, Rakiura Stewart Island and Rēkohu Chatham Islands, and on many offshore islands.

Description: This rosette herb has a short, stout stem with long petiolate leaves up to 27cm long that have 1–5 parallel veins. Hairy peduncles, up to 37cm long, arise from the stout stem at the base of the rosette. Many flowers are densely crowded in a compact inflorescence at the end of the peduncle. At the base of each flower is a pair of small bracts that have a few hairs on the tip only. The flowers, less than 3mm long, are rather inconspicuous. The fruits are dry, oblong capsules, 2–4mm long. Each capsule splits apart around the middle to release the five seeds within.

UREURE
GLASSWORT

Salicornia quinqueflora

This odd-looking plant is also found in mainland Australia and Tasmania. Other species of *Salicornia* are present in North America, Europe, South Africa and South Asia. Ureure and its overseas cousins grow in salt marshes, beaches and mangroves. The common name glasswort is now applied to different species of *Salicornia* but was originally restricted to species in England that were burned to produce sodium carbonate (soda ash), which was used in making glass and soap.

Habitat and distribution: Along coastlines in salt marshes and on rocky and sandy beaches throughout Te Ika-a-Māui North Island, Te Waipounamu South Island, Rakiura Stewart Island as well as Rangitāhua Kermadec Islands and Rēkohu Chatham Islands.

Description: This fleshy herbaceous plant has multiple trailing woody stems about 3–4mm in diameter, each with multiple articulated, erect or ascending branchlets up to 2cm long. The leaves are opposite one another and reduced to tiny scales. They are translucent, fleshy, and green or flushed with red. At each node, the leaves are completely fused to form a cylindrical joint 5–15mm long and 3–7mm wide, but the tip of the leaf is free and forms a collar with two tiny lobes. The flowers appear along a 1–5cm-long inflorescence and are partially covered by bracts. There are 5–10 flowers per whorl. Each flower has 3–4 fused tepals, 1–2 stamens and one style. The fruits are egg-shaped and the seeds are about 2mm long, with a coriaceous coat covered in minute hooked hairs.

KŌKIHI
NEW ZEALAND SPINACH

Tetragonia tetragonoides

Although kōkihi is found throughout Aotearoa, it is restricted to localised pockets. The green leaves can be cooked and eaten like spinach, and Captain James Cook used the plant to prevent scurvy in his crew when he visited Aotearoa. Kōkihi is eaten as a vegetable here and in many other parts of the world, and its seeds have been commercially available since the early 1800s. It is also native to Australia, Japan and southern South America.

Habitat and distribution: Coastal areas, including sandy shorelines, dunes, stony beaches and disturbed areas throughout Te Ika-a-Māui North Island, Te Waipounamu South Island, Rakiura Stewart Island, Rangitāhua Kermadec Islands and Manawatāwhi Three Kings Islands.

Description: A creeping herbaceous plant with branching stems up to 60cm long that lie close to the ground and curve upwards at the tips. The leaves are alternate, borne on petioles up to 2cm long. The leaf blades are heart-shaped or triangular, thick and densely covered with small fleshy bumps, and have smooth or wavy edges. The small flowers are sessile in the leaf axils, found singly or in pairs, and have a yellow corolla about 7mm in diameter. The fruits are hard capsules up to 1cm long, shaped like a spinning top, each with 4–10 horned seeds.

MĀIKUKU
WHITE SUN ORCHID

Thelymitra longifolia

Māikuku is one of the most common and variable terrestrial orchids found in Aotearoa. Since its scientific description and naming more than 250 years ago, at least nine new names have been created and assigned to some of the forms within the species. Current research at Te Papa is using historical herbarium specimens, modern collections and DNA analyses to understand how different these forms are and whether they should be recognised as separate species.

Habitat and distribution: Coastal to subalpine areas ranging from grassy banks, among shrubs under beech forest, and sometimes on roadside verges. Widespread across Te Ika-a-Māui North Island, Te Waipounamu South Island and Rakiura Stewart Island. Also on Manawatāwhi Three Kings Islands, Rēkohu Chatham Islands and Motu Maha Auckland Islands.

Description: This terrestrial orchid reaches up to 50cm tall when flowering. At the base of the flowering stem is a single leaf that is usually thick and strappy, measuring 7–46cm long and 2–2.5cm wide. The inflorescence is erect and rather fleshy, with 1–3 small bracts and 2–15 flowers, and it reaches 30–50cm in length. The flowers are 1–2cm across and have three sepals and three petals. The sepals are green-brownish on the outside and white on the inside, 6–12mm long and 2.5–4mm wide, and have an acute tip. The lateral sepals and the labellum are of a similar shape, white, pointed at the tip, and 6–9mm long and 2–4.5mm wide. The column is 8mm long and topped by a cluster of white hairs and a yellow to dark brown crown.

PŌWHIWHI
NEW ZEALAND BINDWEED

Calystegia tuguriorum

In addition to being native to Aotearoa, pōwhiwhi is also native to mainland Chile and the Juan Fernández Islands. Aotearoa is also home to three other native species of *Calystegia*, as well as one naturalised European species, greater bindweed (*C. sylvatica*). This has much larger flowers and larger, triangular leaves compared with the native species. Because greater bindweed can be invasive, smothering native vegetation, it is important to be able to tell the species apart.

Habitat and distribution: Lowland habitats such as coasts, shrubland, forest margins and disturbed areas. Found throughout Te Ika-a-Māui North Island, Te Waipounamu South Island, Rakiura Stewart Island and Rēkohu Chatham Islands.

Description: A slender, branched, twining vine that arises from a rhizome and scrambles over other vegetation. It can also lie prostrate on the ground. The heart-shaped leaf blades are petiolate, 2–4cm long and 2–3cm wide, with a smooth or wavy edge and a pointed tip. The slender petioles are up to 4cm long. The peduncles supporting the flowers are up to 11cm long, and are cylindrical or winged. The large funnel-shaped flowers can be up to 6cm in diameter and are white or pink. The egg-shaped fruit capsules are about 1cm long and contain orange seeds.

PŌĀNANGA
FORSTER'S CLEMATIS

Clematis forsteri

Pōānanga was described and given a scientific name in 1791 by the German botanist Johann Friedrich Gmelin. Since then, many have referred to *Clematis forsteri* as a 'species complex', meaning that it is possible one or more species are included under the name. Almost 200 years later, Aotearoa botanists demonstrated that the diversity in leaf shape and leaf dissection that characterises *Clematis forsteri* was because some plants actually belonged to another species, *C. petriei*.

Habitat and distribution: Lowland forest areas throughout Te Ika-a-Māui North Island and northern Te Waipounamu South Island.

Description: This evergreen woody vine often climbs over shrubs and small trees. The stems are up to 5m long and 1cm in diameter, ribbed, sparsely hairy when young and hairless when mature. The leaves are 1–6cm long and 1–3cm wide, thin to coriaceous, green to grey-green, and divided into three leaflets. The flowers are 1–5cm in diameter and are solitary or borne in clusters of up to ten in the leaf axil. All surfaces of the flower are moderately to densely hairy. Male and female flowers are on separate plants, and female flowers are generally larger than male flowers. The flowers have 5–6 sepals that are 1–3cm long and up to 1cm wide, elliptic to oblong to egg-shaped, and cream in colour, often flushed red or red-brown at the base. The seeds are 3–4mm long, 1.5mm wide and less than 1mm thick; they are hairy and light to dark brown. Each seed has a long feathery tail that aids dispersal by wind.

KŌHIA
NEW ZEALAND PASSIONFLOWER

Passiflora tetrandra

Of the 500 species of passionflower, most are found in tropical areas of the world; kōhia is the only one endemic to Aotearoa. Some passionflower species are known for their delicious edible passion fruits. Although the small summer fruits of kōhia are not usually eaten by people (they are mostly consumed by birds and possums), they were an important source of fragrant oil to Māori, called hinu kōhia.

Habitat and distribution: Thickets and canopies in lowland and montane forests and forest margins throughout Te Ika-a-Māui North Island and northern Te Waipounamu South Island.

Description: A vigorous, dioecious, glabrous, high-climbing vine that grows on trees in the forest canopy and can reach heights of 15m. The vine's leaves have a smooth edge and are simple, alternate, narrow, pointed, petiolate, dark glossy green above, and about 5–12cm long and 2–4cm wide. The axils of the leaves have long, curved tendrils that help it climb, or 2–3 fragrant flowers clustered into small inflorescences. The flowers are white to yellowish green and less than 2cm wide, with sepals and petals surrounding a ring of thread-like structures. The fruits are round or oblong, about 2–3cm in diameter, and orange with a red oily pulp. Inside, several flattened, wrinkled black seeds can be found.

TĀTARĀMOA
BUSH LAWYER

Rubus australis

The prickles on tātarāmoa are an adaptation that enable it to scramble and climb over other forest plants. They may grab on to you as you walk through the bush and not want to let go, which may be why the species' common English name is bush lawyer. There are six endemic species of *Rubus* in Aotearoa, which can be distinguished by leaf, fruit, prickle and inflorescence characteristics. As in other bramble species worldwide, the fruits are edible to people and birds. Māori also used the bark and leaves as medicines and for trap and construction materials.

Habitat and distribution: Lowland to montane forest, especially swamp forest throughout Te Ika-a-Māui North Island, Te Waipounamu South Island and Rakiura Stewart Island.

Description: A stout, dioecious, scrambling and hook-climbing vine. Juvenile stems are hairy and creep over the forest floor, producing adult stems that can reach more than 10m long. The leaves are up to 5cm long (smaller on juvenile plants) and are each supported by a 2–5cm-long petiole. Each leaf comprises three or five leaflets, which are glabrous and elliptic, egg-shaped or circular, with toothed edges and rounded or pointed tips. The stems, petioles and midrib of the underside of the leaflets are covered in backward-curving hooks or prickles. In spring, the white flowers are arranged in clusters at the ends of branches that are up to 20cm long. In summer, the yellow to red berries, about 1cm in diameter, contain many tiny fruits.

MAKOMAKO
WINEBERRY

Aristotelia serrata

The juicy dark fruit of the endemic makomako – also known as the wineberry – is eaten in summer by kererū and other native birds. People have also found many uses for the leaves, bark and wood of this fast-growing tree, including as medicines for a range of conditions and dyes.

Habitat and distribution: Forms thickets in moist forest clearings throughout Te Ika-a-Māui North Island, Te Waipounamu South Island and Rakiura Stewart Island.

Description: A dioecious shrub or tree up to 10m tall and with a trunk up to 30cm in diameter, makomako has heart-shaped petiolate leaves that are usually found in pairs on the branches. The thin leaf blades are 5–12cm long and 4–8cm wide, with a broad rounded base, a long and pointed tip, and deeply serrated edges. The petiolate leaves are green above and paler green to purplish below, and are mostly glabrous except for some hairs on the veins on the underside only. The small cream to red flowers are clustered into 6–10cm-long branched inflorescences. The fruit is a berry about 5mm in length, can range from bright red to black in colour, and has about eight seeds.

RANGIORA
BUSHMAN'S FRIEND

Brachyglottis repanda

Rangiora is an endemic species in the daisy family (Asteraceae) that flowers in spring. The soft white felt-like underside of the leaves prompted Pākehā settlers to use them as a toilet paper substitute – thus their common English name of bushman's friend. Māori had many other uses for rangiora, including as poultices for sores, gum for bad breath and a food wrap for cooking.

Habitat and distribution: Coastal and lowland forest and shrubland throughout Te Ika-a-Māui North Island and northern Te Waipounamu South Island.

Description: This shrub or tree grows up to 6m tall, with branches covered in white hairs. The leaves are distinctively two-toned, being pale green above and white below thanks to a covering of white hairs. They are petiolate, 5–25cm long and 5–20cm wide, broadest at the base, with toothed to lobed edges. The petioles themselves are up to 10cm long and have a distinct groove. Clusters of about 10–12 tiny, fragrant creamy flowers are arranged into small heads, which in turn are grouped together into much-branched white inflorescences at the tips of the branches. The fruits of rangiora are less than 1mm long, and are topped with a tuft of feathery, hooked hairs up to 3mm long.

TAWA

Beilschmiedia tawa

Tawa was an important source of medicine, food and wood for Māori and for early Pākehā settlers. For instance, the bark was used in an infusion to treat stomach aches and colds, and a decoction of the bark was used to heal wounds. The fruits, which resemble plums, were boiled or steamed before eating, while the large seeds were roasted and sometimes crushed before being consumed. Tawa wood was used for construction (fence rails, shingles), fuel and hunting weapons (spears).

Habitat and distribution: Lowland and low montane forests throughout Te Ika-a-Māui North Island and northern Te Waipounamu South Island.

Description: An evergreen tree that grows up to 35m tall. Its trunk can reach up to 1.2m in diameter and forms buttressed roots when mature. Its bark is smooth and dark brown, often obscured by light-coloured lichens growing on its surface. The leaves are opposite, simple and thinly coriaceous, each held by a petiole up to 1cm long. The leaf laminae are narrow-elliptic, occasionally lance-shaped, 4–7cm long and 1–2cm wide, yellow-green and glabrous above, and bluish green with scattered, pale golden hairs below. The leaf margins are entire and wavy, and the leaf apex is acute or narrowing to a long, sharp point. The flowers are only 2–3mm in diameter, pale green and arranged in a loose cluster about 10cm long. The fruits are egg-shaped, 2–3cm long and 1–1.5cm wide, fleshy, glaucous or shiny, and red, dark purple or almost black when ripe.

KŌWHAI NGUTU-KĀKĀ
KĀKĀ BEAK

Clianthus puniceus

Kōwhai ngutu-kākā is one of New Zealand's rarest plants and currently only one natural population exists in the wild. Browsing and poor seed formation due to the extinction of its bird pollinators are likely to be the main threats to its survival. However, historical accounts from early Pākehā settlers suggest that this species was always rare. These records also note that Māori planted kōwhai ngutu-kākā near kāinga (villages) and used the stunning salmon-red flowers as ear ornaments. Fortunately, this shrub is now common in gardens in Aotearoa and overseas.

Habitat and distribution: Coastal scrub on cliff faces on the east coast of Te Ika-a-Māui North Island.

Description: This multi-stemmed shrub can grow up to 1–2m high and 1–2m wide. The compound leaves measure 8–13cm by 3–5cm, and comprise 14–25 grey-green to olive-green leaflets. Together, the petiole and rachis can be up to 10cm long and 2mm in diameter, and are grooved. Each leaflet lamina is 2–3cm long and less than 1cm wide, elliptic, and rounded at the tip or with a shallow notch. Although up to forty floral buds are produced on each branch, only 4–10 buds fully develop into flowers, which are arranged in a pendulous inflorescence. The calyx is 7–8mm long and 7–8mm wide, light green, and has narrowly triangular lobes. The corolla is salmon pink to red, or rarely light cream to yellow. The fruit is a pod 5–9cm long and 1–2cm wide. The seeds in the pod are 3–4mm long, kidney-shaped, and mottled black and olive green.

KARAMŪ

Coprosma lucida

Karamū is one of the most widespread species of *Coprosma* found in Aotearoa. A few historical records tell us that karamū seeds, and those of other widespread *Coprosma* species, were once investigated as a local alternative to coffee beans. The rationale behind this idea was that *Coprosma* and coffee (genus *Coffea*) both belong to the same plant family, Rubiaceae. In 1877, a note written by explorer, farmer and public servant JC Crawford described karamū coffee as a 'coffee of fine flavour'. The idea, however, did not thrive. Perhaps the scientific name of the genus played against it – *Coprosma* means 'smells like dung', referring to the unpleasant odour produced by the leaves of some species when crushed.

Habitat and distribution: Lowland to montane forest and scrub throughout Te Ika-a-Māui North Island, Te Waipounamu South Island and Rakiura Stewart Island.

Description: This shrub or small tree reaches up to 5m tall. The leaves are opposite on stout glabrous petioles that are 1–3cm long. At the base of the petiole are two short triangular stipules, each with 1–3 small teeth and some hairs. The leaves are thick, coriaceous, glossy dark green above and paler below. The leaf lamina is slightly egg-shaped to broadly elliptic, 12–17cm long and 3–4cm wide, with a raised central main vein. The leaf margin is sometimes wavy. Male and female flowers are on different plants. Male flowers are grouped into dense clusters on simple or branched peduncles 1–1.5cm long. Four to five stamens are contained within a funnel-like corolla. Female flowers are arranged into groups of 3–4 per cluster on branched peduncles. The two styles are long and feather-like, and are also contained within a funnel-shaped corolla. The fruits are orange-red, oblong and about 1cm long.

KARAKA

Corynocarpus laevigatus

The traditional preparation and use of karaka by Māori exemplifies their extensive mātauranga (knowledge) of the natural world and strong connection to the Aotearoa bush. Although the fruits are poisonous, they were an important food source to Māori. An elaborate preparation was required before consumption was possible, including boiling and soaking the fruits for days and then roasting the kernels. Karaka was usually planted around kāinga (villages) and was one of the plants Māori took with them when moving to new areas.

Habitat and distribution: Coastal forests throughout Te Ika-a-Māui North Island and northern Te Waipounamu South Island.

Description: This canopy tree reaches up to 15m tall. Its trunk is up to 6m in diameter and its bark is smooth and grey. The leaves are borne on stout petioles 1–1.5cm long. The leaf lamina is thick, coriaceous, elliptic or oblong, 10–20cm long and 5–7cm wide, dark green and glossy, with recurved margins. The flowers are small, 4–5mm in diameter, and arranged in stout, stiff inflorescences up to 2cm long. The sepals are green and round, and the petals are greenish yellow and spoon-shaped, with small teeth along the margins. The fruits are 2–4cm long, egg-shaped and orange. The seed coat has a distinct reticulated pattern.

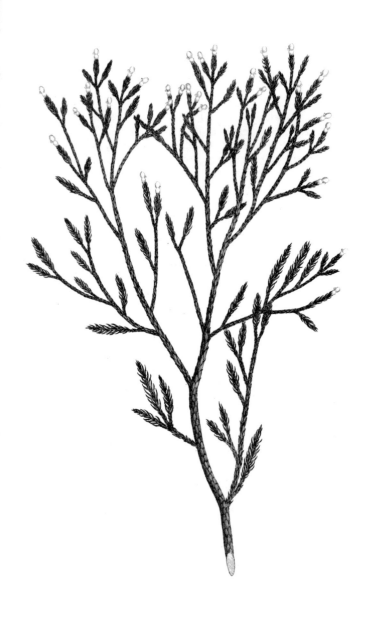

RIMU

Dacrydium cupressinum

In the past, rimu was one of the most important sources of timber in Aotearoa and was widely used for housing, flooring and cabinetmaking. The great quality of its wood led to widespread logging, and old stands of this tree are now uncommon. Today, the government regulates felling of this slow-growing conifer. Interest in the tree has sparked again, this time not because of its wood but for its 'fruit' (technically, this is not a fruit but a female cone covered by a fleshy membrane). Rimu is the most important food for kākāpō, the flightless parrot found only in Aotearoa that is on the brink of extinction. Kākāpō tend to breed only in the years when rimu produce abundant 'fruit'.

Habitat and distribution: Lowland to montane forest throughout Te Ika-a-Māui North Island, Te Waipounamu South Island and Rakiura Stewart Island.

Description: This tree reaches up to 50m in height and its trunk grows up to 2m in diameter. Its bark is dark brown, scaling off in thick flakes. Adult trees have a few main branches with numerous smaller branchlets hanging downwards, giving the crown a distinctive weeping appearance. The leaves are tiny, measuring only 4–7mm long and 1mm wide. They are overlapping, harsh to the touch, olive to reddish green, ridged and linear. Male and female reproductive structures are borne on separate trees. Male cones are solitary or in pairs, and up to 1cm long. Female cones are solitary ovules, up to 4mm long, and located at the end of curved branchlets. Terminal leaves form a swollen red succulent receptacle, where the seed sits. The seed is black, egg-shaped and about 4mm long.

KOHEKOHE
NEW ZEALAND MAHOGANY

Didymocheton spectabilis

Unlike many other trees in Aotearoa, kohekohe has flowers that sprout directly from its trunk and naked branches. This feature is known as cauliflory and is believed to be an adaptation to pollination and seed dispersal by animals or insects that cannot fly or that live at ground level. Unfortunately for kohekohe, introduced animals such as rats and possums can easily reach and eat the fruits, preventing seed production and ultimately regeneration. In 2021, the scientific name for the species was changed from *Dysoxylum spectabile* to *Didymocheton spectabilis*.

Habitat and distribution: Coastal to lowland forest in Te Ika-a-Māui North Island and northern Te Waipounamu South Island.

Description: This tree reaches up to 15m tall and its trunk measures up to 1m in diameter. Its bark is pale brown. The leaves are divided into several leaflets that are arranged in pairs along a central rachis. The leaf lamina is 7–15cm long and 3–4cm wide, slightly oblong, coriaceous, glossy and wavy. The flowers are arranged in clusters that appear directly from the trunk and branches. Some trees produce flowers with both male and female reproductive parts, whereas others produce only male flowers. The flowers are up to 3cm in diameter. The petals are narrow, waxy white, backwards-pointing and up to 1cm long. The stamens are fused together, forming a cylinder around the style. The fruit is an egg-shaped to round fleshy capsule, about 2.5cm long. A fleshy orange to scarlet membrane covers the seeds.

HĪNAU

Elaeocarpus dentatus

There are two varieties of hīnau in Aotearoa, which differ mainly in leaf shape and petiole length. The conservation status of the less common variety (*Elaeocarpus dentatus* var. *obovatus*) is currently considered Data Deficient; this means that the species could be threatened but there is not enough information about its distribution or abundance to make a well-informed decision. An interesting feature of the adult leaves of hīnau is the presence of domatia, small pouch-like cavities found along the midrib of the leaf. It is believed that mites use these structures to hide from predators, and in exchange the plant receives protection from fungi or herbivorous mites.

Habitat and distribution: Coastal to lowland forest in Te Ika-a-Māui North Island and Te Waipounamu South Island.

Description: This canopy tree reaches more than 15m tall and its trunk is up to 1m in diameter. The bark is grey and smooth. The leaves are held on stout petioles up to 2.5cm long. The leaf lamina is 10–12cm long by 2–3cm wide, oblong with a rounded or pointed tip, coriaceous and with whitish silky hairs underneath. The leaf margin can be wavy, recurved or bluntly toothed. Flowers face downwards and are arranged into long inflorescences about 10cm long, each with 8–12 flowers held by silky-hairy pedicels 1cm long. The flowers are 1–1.5cm across, with 3–5-lobed white petals that are almost 1cm long. The sepals are about 6mm long, narrowly oblong and with hairs on their external surface. The fruits are 1–2cm long and 1cm wide, egg-shaped, and purplish when mature.

WHAU
NEW ZEALAND CORK TREE

Entelea arborescens

Whau is a very fast-growing tree in the mallow family (Malvaceae). Its wood is very light and was used by Māori for making pōito (fishing floats), kārewa (buoys) and mōkihi (rafts). Because of its great buoyancy, whau is also called the New Zealand cork tree. It has been suggested that the species' current geographical distribution is the result of pre-European cultivation by Māori. However, genetic studies led by Te Papa scientists have looked into this hypothesis and discovered that there is no genetic evidence to support it.

Habitat and distribution: Coastal to lowland forest and shrubland, usually on forest margins or in disturbed areas. Found on Manawatāwhi Three Kings Islands, Te Ika-a-Māui North Island and Te Waipounamu South Island.

Description: This shrub or small tree grows up to 6m tall with a trunk up to 25cm in diameter. Its bark is grey, and the branchlets, leaves and petioles are covered in soft whitish hairs. The leaves are bright green and alternate, and held on petioles up to 3cm long. The leaf lamina is 10–28cm long and 19–26cm wide. It is wide with a saw-like margin that is doubly notched with forward-pointing teeth, a heart-shaped base and a sharp, tapering apex. Multiple flowers are arranged in an inflorescence. The flowers have four sepals that are slightly hairy, with a pointed, tapering tip, and 4–5 wrinkled white petals. The stamens are numerous and bright yellow. The fruits are almost spherical, about 2cm across, and covered in rather rigid, spiny hairs that are 1.5–2.5cm long.

KŌTUKUTUKU
TREE FUCHSIA

Fuchsia excorticata

Four features make kōtukutuku quite an unusual species: it is the largest species of fuchsia in the world; it has blue pollen; it is one of the few trees in Aotearoa that loses its leaves over winter; and its flowers change colour from green to red. Red flowers have no nectar and are ignored by pollinators – birds such as tūī and korimako (bellbird). The direction of this colour change challenges the notion that birds are mostly attracted to red flowers.

Habitat and distribution: Lowland and lower montane forest, near forest margins and along streams throughout Te Ika-a-Māui North Island, Te Waipounamu South Island and Rakiura Stewart Island. Also on offshore islands such as Motu Maha Auckland Islands and Rēkohu Chatham Islands.

Description: This deciduous tree reaches up to 12m tall. Its papery bark is light pink or brownish orange and peels in strips. The leaves are thin, dark green above and pale bluish green to silvery below, and are held on slender, 1–4cm-long petioles. The leaf lamina is 2–14cm long and 1–7cm wide, elliptical or oblong, usually wavy, and mostly hairless except on the veins and margins. The flowers are usually solitary and pendulous, and often appear directly from the branches or trunks on thin pedicels that are 1–2cm long. The floral tube is 1–2cm long and green to purple at first, turning red. The sepals are 0.5–1.5cm long and green at first, before the whole calyx turns red. The petals are less than 0.5cm long, dark purple and elliptic. The stamens are purple and extend beyond the floral tube on 1cm-long filaments. The style is 2–3.5cm long, almost the same size as the stamens. The fruits are 1cm long, oblong, and dark purple to almost black.

TĀWINIWINI
BUSH SNOWBERRY

Gaultheria antipoda

The fruits of the endemic tāwiniwini appear in summer and look like berries, hence the common English name for the species being bush snowberry. However, they are not true berries in the botanical sense, because the fleshy part develops from the calyx and not from the ovary. Snowberry fruits can be white or red, and are eaten by skinks, wētā, birds such as kea, and humans.

Habitat and distribution: Widespread in montane to subalpine areas, especially in rocky habitats throughout Te Ika-a-Māui North Island, Te Waipounamu South Island and Rakiura Stewart Island.

Description: This spreading shrub reaches 0.5–2m in height. The leaves have tiny hairy petioles that are alternate along the branch. The leaf blades are glabrous, leathery and egg-shaped, and have wavy to toothed margins and a rounded or pointed tip. The leaf blades are about 1cm long by 1cm wide, but become smaller towards the branch tips. The flowers are found individually in the axils of the leaves, and are suspended on hairy pedicels. The white corolla is urn-shaped and topped with triangular lobes that curve upwards. The corolla is surrounded by a calyx that is deeply cut into five pointed triangular lobes. During fruiting, the calyx enlarges up to 1cm in diameter to become a plump, fleshy white to red covering for the dry fruit inside.

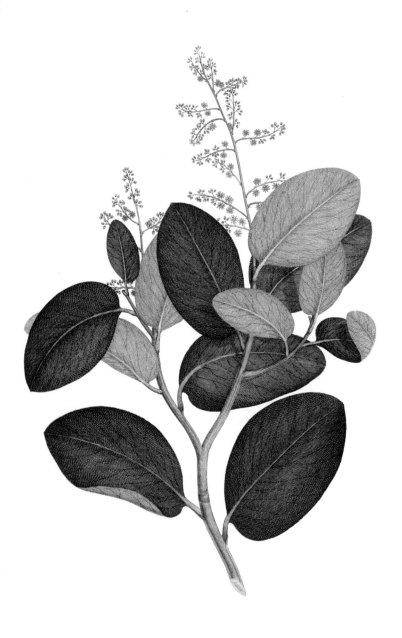

PUKA
SHINING BROADLEAF

Griselinia lucida

Puka starts its life growing high up in the canopy of other trees. This species is considered a hemi-epiphyte (a plant that spends only part of its life cycle as an epiphyte) because after a few years it sends roots all the way down to the forest floor and becomes self-sufficient. The roots grow down rapidly (about 1.2m per year) and when they reach the soil they provide the plant with access to water and nutrients, which may not be abundant up in the forest canopy.

Habitat and distribution: Usually grows as an epiphyte on trees in lowland forest, or terrestrially in coastal areas throughout Te Ika-a-Māui North Island and Te Waipounamu South Island.

Description: This shrub or tree grows up to 8m tall. It usually begins its life by perching on tree branches, developing long roots that descend to the soil. Its bark is thick and has furrows that run longitudinally. The leaves are 7–17cm long, leathery and very glossy. The leaf lamina is broadly egg-shaped, with a round apex, and unequally heart-shaped at the base. The midrib and other main veins are prominent in the underside of the leaf. Male and female flowers are on different plants. The flowers are very small and greenish. Male flowers have five sepals that are 1–2mm long and five petals that are 2–3mm long. Female flowers have five highly reduced sepals and no petals. The fruits are fleshy, dark purple and up to 1cm long.

REWAREWA
NEW ZEALAND HONEYSUCKLE

Knightia excelsa

Rewarewa is one of New Zealand's tallest trees. It is one of only two species in the protea family (Proteaceae) in Aotearoa, most members of which occur in Australia, South Africa and South America. Unlike in other flowers, the female part of the rewarewa flower helps to distribute the pollen. Specifically, the stamens of rewarewa deposit their pollen directly on a particular area of the immature, non-receptive stigma. As birds drink nectar from the flowers, they brush off the pollen from the stigma and transfer it to other flowers on the same or another tree.

Habitat and distribution: Coastal, lowland and montane forest. Common in regenerating forest in Te Ika-a-Māui North Island and northern Te Waipounamu South Island.

Description: This slender tree reaches up to 30m tall and its trunk is more than 1m in diameter. Smaller branches are covered in rust-coloured hairs. Leaves of juvenile trees are thinly coriaceous, up to 30cm long, narrow and tapering, and acutely saw-like. The leaves of adult trees are very thick, 10–15cm long and 2.5–4cm wide, and are carried on stout petioles about 1cm long. The leaf lamina is narrow and oblong, rigid, coarsely saw-like, covered in fine hairs when young and glabrous when mature. The flowers are arranged in compact clusters up to 10cm long. The corollas are dark red, long and slender. The fruits are 3–4cm long and split open on one side when dry to release the seeds. The seeds are almost 1cm long and each has a wing about 1.5cm long that assists in wind dispersal.

RAMARAMA

Lophomyrtus bullata

Ramarama is an endemic tree that is common and widespread in Aotearoa forests. Its small berries are attractive to birds from late summer to early winter. Alarmingly, the species is now seriously threatened. These trees are very susceptible to myrtle rust, a pathogenic fungus from South America that arrived in Australia in 2010 and Aotearoa in 2017.

Habitat and distribution: Coastal and lowland forests throughout Te Ika-a-Māui North Island and northern Te Waipounamu South Island.

Description: A shrub or tree that grows to more than 6m tall. The evergreen leaves are short-petiolate and arranged in pairs along the branches. The leaf blades are bronze-green with red spots, shiny and with a blistered appearance, thick, around 2–4cm long and 1–2cm wide, and broad-oval in shape with a rounded or pointed tip. Each flower has two tiny bracts and arises singly from the leaf axil on a 2cm-long peduncle. The four circular white petal lobes form a flat, spreading corolla about 1cm in diameter, from which dozens of white stamens project upwards. The ramarama fruit is a red to black egg-shaped berry less than 1cm long with many seeds.

MĀHOE

Melicytus ramiflorus

Māhoe belongs to the violet family (Violaceae). Its wood is very light and soft, and it was used by Māori when lighting fires using friction. In this method, a pointy stick of kaikōmako (*Pennantia corymbosa*) was rubbed against a māhoe board until a groove was created. Eventually, an ember formed at the end of the groove, at which point dry material was added to start a fire. In Māori mythology, māhoe and kaikōmako are two of the five tree species on which Mahuika, the goddess of fire, inadvertently deposited a small amount of fire while trying to discipline her grandson Māui, the trickster.

Habitat and distribution: Coastal and lowland forests throughout Te Ika-a-Māui North Island and Te Waipounamu South Island. Also on Rangitāhua Kermadec Islands.

Description: This tree grows up to 10m tall and has whitish bark. It is sometimes multi-branched at the base and has dense foliage. The leaves are carried on slender petioles about 2cm long. The leaf lamina is elliptic, 5–15cm long and 3–5cm wide, slightly membranaceous, and with a coarsely toothed, saw-like margin. The leaf base is tapering, while the apex can be rounded, pointed or tapering to a sharp tip (all forms may be found on the same plant). Male and female flowers occur on different trees. The solitary flowers are 3–4mm in diameter, borne on slender pedicels 5–10mm long and sprouting in clusters directly from the branches. The petals are yellow in male flowers and greenish in female flowers. The fruits are violet to dark blue or purplish, 4–5mm long, and egg-shaped to spherical; they each contain 3–6 seeds.

PŌHUTUKAWA
NEW ZEALAND CHRISTMAS TREE

Metrosideros excelsa

Pōhutukawa is of high cultural importance to Māori and Pākehā alike. It is one of twelve species in the genus *Metrosideros* endemic to Aotearoa, half of which are trees or shrubs and the other half of which are climbing vines. Like many other species in the myrtle family (Myrtaceae), pōhutukawa is susceptible to myrtle rust and is now considered to be threatened. Habitat loss and browsing by possums are additional threats to this iconic tree.

Habitat and distribution: Coastal forests and on the shores of inland lakes. Native to Te Ika-a-Māui North Island, but naturally found in the upper half only, and widely planted further south.

Description: A tree with multiple spreading, stout trunks and branches, which can grow up to 20m tall with an even wider crown. The evergreen leaves are short-petiolate and arranged in pairs along the branches. The leaf blades are thick, leathery, dark green, 5–10cm long and 2.5–5cm wide, and oblong with a rounded or pointed tip. The underside of the leaf surface has a covering of short white velvety hairs. Many flowers are clustered together into brush-like inflorescences. Each flower has five crimson petals and a few dozen crimson stamens about 4cm long, which give the flower its bristly appearance. The fruit of the pōhutukawa is a dry, hairy capsule up to 1cm long, which splits open to release hundreds of seeds.

NGAIO

Myoporum laetum

The endemic ngaio is a hardy tree with evergreen leaves that can tolerate salty, exposed coastal conditions. It has flowers in spring and summer, and fruits through to winter. The dots on the leaves – known as pellucid glands – are best seen when holding the leaf up to the light. These glands produce an oil that contains ngaione, which, perhaps paradoxically, can be both poisonous (it is a liver toxin to most farm stock) and medicinal. The bark and leaves have been used for toothaches, skin ailments and as insect repellents for mosquitoes and sand flies.

Habitat and distribution: Coastal and lowland forests, especially on forest margins. On Te Ika-a-Māui North Island, Te Waipounamu South Island (but rare in the lower half) and Rēkohu Chatham Islands. Also on Rangitāhua Kermadec Islands and Manawatāwhi Three Kings Islands.

Description: A low-growing shrub or tree up to 10m tall with a stout trunk and branches. The bark is rough, brown and furrowed. The leaves have petioles about 1–2cm long, and large laminae 4–14cm long and 1–5cm wide that are elliptic, narrowing to the base and to a pointed tip. The laminae are hairless, thick, fleshy and bright green, dotted with white or yellow glands. Up to six flowers, each borne on a short pedicel, are clustered together in the leaf axils. Each flower has a bell-shaped corolla about 1cm in diameter that is white with purple spots and hairy inside. The fruits are narrowly egg-shaped, up to 1cm long and red to purple.

MĀPOU

Myrsine australis

Māpou is an endemic tree found in forest understoreys and produces clusters of tiny flowers and fruits from spring to late summer. The fruits are eaten by many native birds, including kererū, tūī and korimako (bellbird), which disperse the seeds. The wavy-edged, light green leaves borne on distinctive red branches make the species easy to identify in Aotearoa forests.

Habitat and distribution: Lowland to montane forests, especially on forest margins throughout Te Ika-a-Māui North Island, Te Waipounamu South Island and Rakiura Stewart Island.

Description: A dioecious shrub or small tree up to 6m tall, with dark bark that is red on young branches. The short-petiolate leaves have leathery laminae that are 3–6cm long and 2–3cm wide, light green, oblong with rounded tips, and with wavy margins. The flowers have short pedicels and are clustered into crowded inflorescences in the leaf axils; they are less than 3mm across, white, and have four petals and four sepals. Male flowers have four stamens with large anthers (which produce pollen) but a shrivelled ovary, whereas female flowers have a functional ovary but sterile anthers (which do not have pollen). The small round to oval fruits are 2–3mm in diameter and dark brown to black.

PINĀTORO
NEW ZEALAND DAPHNE

Pimelea prostrata

The endemic pinātoro is commonly planted as a groundcover in gardens, where it forms attractive blue-green carpets with sweet-scented star-like flowers and acts as both shelter and a food source for native lizards. It flowers and fruits for most of the year, from September to April. Since the species was first formally described by European botanists in the late eighteenth century, several subspecies have been named. These can be distinguished by minor differences in their features, habitat preferences and distribution.

Habitat and distribution: Coastal to subalpine zones in rocky or gravelly areas, including a range of open habitats such as river terraces, grassland, open shrubland and fellfields throughout Te Ika-a-Māui North Island and Te Waipounamu South Island.

Description: A sprawling, branched evergreen shrub that grows flat along the ground, forming mats up to 1m wide. Its main branches are stout and dark brown to black, whereas young branches are more slender, flexible and hairy. The many small, sessile blue-green leaves are packed quite close to one another along the branches. The leaf blades are up to 6mm long and 3mm wide, oblong and leathery, and have red edges. Heads of 3–10 flowers are clustered near the branch tips. The flowers are small, white, hairy and sweet-scented. The small fruits look like oblong berries and can be white or red.

KAWAKAWA
PEPPER TREE

Piper excelsum

Traditionally, kawakawa has been an important medicinal plant for Māori, used to treat a range of ailments. For instance, whole leaves were chewed to relieve toothache, pulped leaves were applied to swollen joints, and a decoction of the leaves was consumed to calm stomach pain. The use of kawakawa has expanded beyond rongoā Māori (traditional Māori healing) and today this plant is used in tea, chocolate, ice cream and even gin. Kawakawa also has a spiritual significance for Māori: the large heart-shaped leaves are a symbol of courage and fortitude. Kawakawa belongs to the pepper family (Piperaceae) and its common Māori name refers to the pungent taste of its leaves (kawa means 'bitter').

Habitat and distribution: Coastal to lowland forest throughout Te Ika-a-Māui North Island and Te Waipounamu South Island.

Description: This shrub or small tree is up to 6m tall. The branches are arranged in a zigzag fashion, with swollen nodes at the points where leaves and branches attach. The leaves are held on petioles 1–4cm long. The leaf lamina is heart-shaped, fleshy, dark green to yellowish green, 5–10cm long and 6–12cm wide, and with a smooth margin. Male and female flowers occur on different plants. The sessile flowers are very small (2–3mm in diameter), with no sepals or petals, and are tightly packed into a short inflorescence. The fleshy yellow or orange fruits are 2–3mm in diameter and somewhat angled.

KŌHŪHŪ

Pittosporum tenuifolium

The endemic kōhūhū belongs to the genus *Pittosporum*, which means 'pitch-seeded' and refers to the sticky gum that surrounds the dark seeds inside the capsules. Birds, moths and other insects are attracted to both the fragrant flowers (in spring) and the fruits (in summer). The sticky substance in the fruits allows the seeds to adhere to the visiting animals, which then act as seed dispersers.

Habitat and distribution: Coastal to lower montane forest throughout Te Ika-a-Māui North Island and in Te Waipounamu South Island apart from western areas.

Description: This tree grows up to 8m tall, with a slender trunk and dark grey bark. Young branches and leaves are hairy. The leaves are alternate and short-petiolate. The leaf blades are smooth, glossy, leathery, pale green, oblong with a pointed tip and smooth but wavy margins, and about 3cm long and 1–2cm wide. The flowers occur singly or in small groups in the leaf axils. The corollas are very dark red, with five spreading petals, each 1cm long. The fruits are spherical, slightly woody capsules about 1cm in diameter. When mature, the fruit turns black and splits open to reveal the black seeds set in a sticky gum.

WHAUWHAUPAKU
FIVE FINGER

Pseudopanax arboreus

Whauwhaupaku is similar to patē (seven finger; see page 107) but has fewer, shinier and thicker leaflets with larger teeth. This endemic tree also produces flowers and fruits earlier than patē, flowering in winter and fruiting the following year in spring to summer.

Habitat and distribution: Lowland forests throughout Te Ika-a-Māui North Island and Te Waipounamu South Island.

Description: A dioecious tree up to 8m tall with spreading branches and large, compound petiolate leaves. Each leaf comprises 5–7 leaflets, each attached to the petiole at a single point at the base of the leaf. The petioles are about 10–20cm long, and the petiolules at the base of the leaflets are 3–5cm long. The thick, glossy green leathery leaflets can be up to 20cm long, and are coarsely and regularly toothed along their edges. The whitish-green flowers are arranged in clusters of 10–15 in small umbrella-like inflorescences, which are in turn arranged into larger inflorescences on red to purple stalks. The flowers on one plant are either all male or all female. The dark fruits on female plants are less than 1cm in diameter, and round but compressed.

KĀMAHI

Pterophylla racemosa

Kāmahi is endemic to Aotearoa and is our most abundant forest tree. It may start life as an epiphyte growing on a tree fern, and its juvenile leaves differ from the undivided adult leaves by having three leaflets each. The bark has a high percentage of tannins, and has been used medicinally as a laxative and also as a dye for tanning. In 2021, the species' scientific name was changed from *Weinmannia racemosa* to *Pterophylla racemosa*.

Habitat and distribution: Lowland to montane forests throughout Te Ika-a-Māui North Island, Te Waipounamu South Island and Rakiura Stewart Island.

Description: An evergreen shrub or large tree up to 25m tall, with wide, irregular, often multiple trunks. The leaves are up to 10cm long and 4cm wide, carried on petioles up to 2cm long. The leaf blades are leathery and elliptic, and coarsely toothed on the edges. At the tips of the branches, dozens of flowers are tightly packed into long, erect, spiky inflorescences up to 12cm long. Each flower is small, with white to pink petals and many stamens that stick out. The fruits are capsules about 5mm long with hairy seeds.

TAUREPO
NEW ZEALAND GLOXINIA

Rhabdothamnus solandri

There are no other species of *Rhabdothamnus* in the world, which means that taurepo is not only an endemic species in Aotearoa, but also an endemic genus! The showy, colourful flowers are produced year-round and contain lots of nectar, which attracts birds. Taurepo are completely dependent on native birds – especially korimako (bellbird), tūī and hihi (stitchbird) – for cross-pollination. Compared with plants on predator-free offshore islands, where these native birds are present, mainland taurepo cannot reproduce because the bird populations here have either decreased or disappeared altogether due to predation by rats and stoats. This is one example of how efforts to control or eradicate introduced predators protect not only birds but also plants.

Habitat and distribution: Coastal and lowland forests, especially in shade near rocks and streams. On Te Ika-a-Māui North Island only, including several nearby offshore islands.

Description: A much-branched, slender, tangled shrub with bristly hairs that grows up to 2m tall. The leaves are carried on 1cm-long petioles. The leaf blades are grey-green with dark veins, hairy, oval to round, 2–3cm long and 2–3cm wide, and with coarse teeth on the edges. The tubular flowers are nodding, about 2–3cm long, and borne singly along the branches on pedicels that are about 2cm long. The showy orange corollas have red stripes and spreading lobes. The fruits are capsules up to 1cm long, egg-shaped, with many small seeds.

PATĒ
SEVEN FINGER

Schefflera digitata

Patē flowers and fruits in late summer. Different parts of this endemic tree are useful as antifungal medicine (the leaves), fire starters and building and craft materials (the wood), and dye (the fruits). The plant is also the main host of pua o te rēinga (*Dactylanthus taylorii*), an unusual threatened, endemic flowering plant that parasitises the roots of patē and a few other native trees and shrubs.

Habitat and distribution: Damp, shady lowland forests throughout Te Ika-a-Māui North Island, Te Waipounamu South Island and Rakiura Stewart Island.

Description: A small, many-branched tree up to 8m tall, patē has large petiolate leaves, with 3–9 leaflets attached to the petiole at a single point. The petioles are up to 25cm long and the petiolules up to 2cm long. The soft, thin green leaflets themselves are up to 20cm long and have numerous small, sharp teeth along their edges. The many flowers are arranged in spreading, branched compound inflorescences up to 35cm long. The greenish flowers are small and only about 7mm in diameter, whereas the dark violet fruits are about half that size, fleshy and spherical.

POROPORO

Solanum aviculare

Poroporo belongs to the nightshade family (Solanaceae) and, as is the case with many other species in this family, contains toxic compounds. Unripe poroporo fruits and leaves are poisonous. Nevertheless, the species has been cultivated overseas and used to produce contraceptives. Some historical records also suggest that ripe fruits were collected by early Pākehā settlers in the Wellington area and used to make jam. The woody stems were used by Māori to make kōauau (flutes).

Habitat and distribution: Coastal forests throughout Te Ika-a-Māui North Island, Te Waipounamu South Island and Rakiura Stewart Island. Also on Rangitāhua Kermadec Islands and Rēkohu Chatham Islands.

Description: This soft-wooded shrub reaches up to 3m tall. The stems are angular and green or purplish. The leaves are dark green, slightly fleshy and carried on 7–35cm-long petioles. The leaf margin is variable, and can range from smooth and unlobed to lobed within the same plant. The leaf lamina is 2–10cm wide; the leaf base extends down the length of the petiole, and the tip tapers to a sharp point. The inflorescences are held on peduncles up to 12cm long and have 2–12 flowers. The calyx is 4–7mm long, with triangular lobes. The corolla is 2.5–3.5cm in diameter and usually mauve, becoming paler towards the margins, or occasionally white. The anthers are 3–4mm long and bright orange. The fruits are 1.5–2.5cm long, broadly egg-shaped, orange and held on drooping pedicels.

KŌWHAI

Sophora tetraptera

Kōwhai is one of New Zealand's best-known native trees and is considered by some to be the national flower. It flowers profusely in spring, providing an important source of nectar to native birds such as tūī and korimako (bellbird). Despite the popularity of kōwhai in city gardens, wild populations have been badly affected by habitat destruction due to forest clearing, poor seed formation due to the scarcity of native bird pollinators, and low regeneration rates due to browsing by introduced animals.

Habitat and distribution: Coastal cliff faces and lowlands to montane forest, mostly near streams or forest margins throughout Te Ika-a-Māui North Island and Te Waipounamu South Island.

Description: A moderate to large tree up to 25m high, with weeping, spreading and ascending branches. The leaves are up to 15cm long, slightly hairy, compound, and with 30–50 light green to green leaflets. On adult trees the leaflets are 4–13mm long and 2–6mm wide, elliptic, slightly egg-shaped and sometimes orbicular. The leaflet apex is rounded and sometimes notched, and the base is tapering to rounded. There are seven flowers clustered in each inflorescence, each flower borne on a pedicel up to 16mm long. The calyx is 5–11mm long and 7–10mm wide, cup-shaped and with a shallowly lobed rim. The corolla is yellow and up to 5cm long. The fruits are nearly-segmented pods 5–20cm long, four-winged, brown and slightly hairy, with up to twelve seeds. The seeds are up to 1cm long and 0.5cm wide, oblong, and light yellow to brown.

ONGAONGA
TREE NETTLE

Urtica ferox

If you encounter this endemic plant in the bush, watch out: *ferox* means 'fierce'! If you brush against the needle-like hairs, you may feel a painful sting, followed by numbness, caused by the toxins they contain. Ongaonga is not toxic to all animals, however. As the primary host plant of the native kahukura (New Zealand red admiral butterfly), it has an important ecological role. Kahukura caterpillars live on ongaonga, eating the leaves and using them for protection.

Habitat and distribution: Bush margins, thickets, forest openings and regenerating forest throughout Te Ika-a-Māui North Island and northern Te Waipounamu South Island.

Description: This branching dioecious shrub is up to 2m tall that may form dense thickets. The leaves, branches and inflorescences are copiously covered in stalked stinging hairs. Along the branches, the leaves are found in pairs and have long petioles. The leaf blades are pointed, triangular, sharply toothed, pale green, and 8–12cm long and 3–5cm wide. The small, inconspicuous flowers are only about 1–2mm across and have tepals and stamens arranged in fours. The flowers are arranged into tassels of branched inflorescences up to 8cm long that dangle from the base of the leaves. The dry brown fruits are equally small – about 1–2mm long.

KOROMIKO

Veronica salicifolia

There are about 125 native species of hebe in Aotearoa, including creeping herbs, alpine cushions, shrubs and small trees. Koromiko is a common lowland shrub that is not only beautiful but also useful, the leaves and shoots having medicinal properties. Leaves from this species and a few other close relatives were shipped to Europe as a popular treatment for curing dysentery in soldiers during the Second World War.

Habitat and distribution: Open lowland sites, from sea level to the treeline, and in lowland forests. Common throughout Te Waipounamu South Island, Rakiura Stewart Island and Motu Maha Auckland Islands.

Description: This openly branched, bushy shrub is up to 2.5m tall and has long, tapering, petiolate and mostly glabrous leaves that are 6–11cm long and 1–2cm wide. The leaf buds have a distinct oblong sinus. Around 100–250 flowers are closely packed into simple lateral, unbranched inflorescences that extend past the leaves. The inflorescences are attached to the branch by a 1–4cm-long peduncle and are themselves up to 20cm long. The flowers have short pedicels and narrow, hairy bracts. The corollas are white or pale lilac, with pointed corolla lobes that are 4mm long and a corolla tube that is longer than the calyx. The fruits of this species are dry, rounded, glabrous capsules that are shorter than the calyx, up to 3.5mm long.

GLOSSARY
REFERENCES
IMAGE CREDITS
ACKNOWLEDGEMENTS

GLOSSARY

Alternate Leaves or other plant structures growing along the stem singly at different intervals, i.e. first on one side and then the other, but not directly opposite.

Anther The terminal part of a stamen that produces and releases pollen.

Axil The upper angle formed between a leaf and the stem from which it grows.

Bract A leaf-like plant structure, usually found at the base of a flower or inflorescence.

Calyx The outermost whorl of a flower, referring to all of the sepals of a flower collectively. See also *corolla; whorl.*

Column A structure formed by the fusion of the male and female reproductive organs; a feature common in orchid flowers.

Compound leaf A leaf composed of a number of leaflets.

Coriaceous Thick, leather-like; mainly used to describe leaves. See also *membranaceous.*

Corolla The second outermost whorl of a flower, referring to all of the petals of a flower collectively. See also *calyx; whorl.*

Cross-pollination The transfer of pollen from the anthers of one flower to the stigma of another flower on a different plant; this may occur via wind or a specialised pollinator such as an insect or bird.

Dioecious A plant species that has male and female reproductive organs in separate flowers on separate individuals.

Domatium (pl. domatia) A small chamber or cavity on a plant leaf that houses small bugs such as mites.

Endemic Indigenous to a specific country or exclusive to a particular place, e.g. a species that is found only in New Zealand and nowhere else. See also *native.*

Epiphyte A plant that grows perching on another plant but is not parasitic. See also *parasite*.

Filament The stalk in the male reproductive organ of a flower (stamen) that holds up the anther. See also *anther; stamen*.

Glabrous Without hairs, smooth.

Glandular hair A plant hair with modified cells, often in a cluster near the tip, that can produce secretions.

Inflorescence A cluster of flowers arranged on a stem in a specific pattern. See also *pedicel; peduncle*.

Labellum The central petal of orchid flowers. This is usually highly modified and serves as the landing platform for pollinators.

Lamina (pl. laminae) Blade (of a leaf).

Leaflet A small leaf-like structure that is one of many in a compound leaf. See also *compound leaf; pinna; pinnate*.

Frond The lamina and petiole of a fern; fronds are often pinnately compound.

Fruit A mature, ripened ovary that bears seeds and is formed after pollination of the flowers.

Margin Edge; often used when discussing leaves.

Membranaceous Thin, soft, pliable, skin-like; mainly used to describe leaves. See also *coriaceous*.

Native Indigenous to a particular location and surrounding areas; e.g. a species that is naturally found in both Australia and New Zealand is native to both countries. See also *endemic*.

Parasite An organism that benefits from an individual of another species (its host) by living on or inside it and getting nutrients from it. See also *epiphyte*.

Pedicel The stalk supporting a flower in an inflorescence. See also *inflorescence; peduncle*.

Peduncle The stalk supporting an inflorescence, or a solitary flower or fruit.

Petal A leaf-like structure in the second outermost whorl of a flower; it is often the colourful part of the flower. See also *calyx; corolla; sepal; tepal; whorl.*

Petiolate Describing a leaf that has a petiole. See also *petiole; sessile.*

Petiole The stalk at the base of a leaf blade attaching it to the stem.

Petiolule The stalk at the base of a leaflet. See also *compound leaf.*

Pinna (pl. pinnae) A leaflet in a pinnately compound leaf; commonly used in ferns to describe the primary division of a frond.

Pinnate Describing a compound leaf that has pinna. See also *compound leaf; pinnae.*

Rachis The main axis of a compound structure, such as a compound leaf, a pinnate fern frond or an inflorescence.

Recurved Bent or curved downwards or outwards.

Rhizome A horizontal underground stem of a plant, which may send out roots and shoots at intervals. See also *stolon.*

Rosette Leaves arranged into a circle, often sitting near the soil.

Sepal An often green, leaf-like structure in the outermost whorl of a flower. See also *calyx; corolla; petal; tepal; whorl.*

Sessile Describing a plant part that lacks a stalk. See also *petiolate.*

Sinus An indentation between two teeth; usually used when describing the margin of a leaf.

Sorus (pl. sori) A cluster of spore-producing organs on the undersurface of some fern fronds.

Stamen The male reproductive organ of a flower, including the filament and anther. See also *anther; filament.*

Stigma The tip of the female reproductive organ of a flower, which receives pollen from the male reproductive organ.

Stipule A leaf-like appendage usually found in pairs near the base of the petiole.

Stolon A horizontal above-ground stem of a plant, which may send out roots and shoots at intervals. See also *rhizome.*

Style The long, narrow stalk-like part of the female reproductive organ of a flower that connects the stigma and the ovary.

Tendril A long, thin, leafless, thread-like appendage in climbing plants such as vines, allowing them to twine around or attach themselves to other plants or objects for support.

Tepal A leaf-like structure in the outermost whorl of a flower that cannot be differentiated into a petal or a sepal. See also *calyx; corolla; petal; sepal; whorl.*

Whorl A radial and circular arrangement of three or more plant parts around a stem; often used when describing flower parts or leaves. See also *calyx; corolla; petal; sepal; tepal.*

REFERENCES

GENERAL

AVH 2022. Australasian Virtual Herbarium, Council of Heads of Australasian Herbaria, avh.chah.org.au, accessed 3 May 2022.

'Banks and Solander black and white engravings', Te Papa Collections Online, collections.tepapa.govt.nz/topic/5507, accessed 3 May 2022.

Beever, J, *A Dictionary of Maori Plant Names*, Auckland Botanical Society, Auckland, 1991.

Crowe, A, *A Field Guide to the Native Edible Plants of New Zealand*, Penguin (NZ), Auckland, 2004.

Gibbs, G, *Ghosts of Gondwana: The History of Life in New Zealand*, Craig Potton Publishing, Nelson, 2006.

de Lange, PJ, JR Rolfe, JW Barkla, SP Courtney, PD Champion, LR Perrie, SM Beadel, KA Ford, I Breitwieser, I Schönberger, R Hindmarsh-Walls, PB Heenan and K Ladley, *Conservation Status of New Zealand Indigenous Vascular Plants*, New Zealand Threat Classification Series, no. 22, Department of Conservation, Wellington, 2018, doc.govt.nz/Documents/science-and-technical/nztcs22entire.pdf, accessed 3 May 2022.

Mabberley, D, M Gooding and J Studholme, *Joseph Banks' Florilegium: Botanical Treasures from Cook's First Voyage*, Thames & Hudson, London, 2017.

Manaaki Whenua – Landcare Research (2022), Ngā Rauropi Whakaoranga, rauropiwhakaoranga.landcareresearch.co.nz, accessed 15 June 2022.

Manaaki Whenua – Landcare Research (2022), Ngā Tipu o Aotearoa – New Zealand Plants Names, biotanz.landcareresearch.co.nz, accessed 15 June 2022.

Schönberger, I, AD Wilton, KF Boardman, I Breitwieser, P de Lange, B de Pauw, KA Ford, ES Gibb, DS Glenny, PA Greer, PB Heenan, MA Korver, HG Maule, PM Novis, JM Prebble, RD Smissen and K Tawiri, *Checklist of the New Zealand Flora – Seed Plants*, Manaaki Whenua – Landcare Research, Lincoln, 2021, dx.doi.org/10.26065/ax7t-8y85, accessed 3 May 2021.

Schönberger, I, AD Wilton, PJ Brownsey, LR Perrie, KF Boardman, I Breitwieser, B de Pauw, KA Ford, ES Gibb, DS Glenny, PA Greer, PB Heenan, MA Korver, HG Maule, PM Novis, JM Prebble, RD Smissen and K Tawiri, *Checklist of the New Zealand Flora – Ferns and Lycophytes*, Manaaki Whenua

– Landcare Research, Lincoln, 2022, dx.doi.org/10.26065/10v5-8469, accessed 3 May 2022.

Schortemeyer, M, JR Evans, D Bruhn, DM Bergstrom and MC Ball, 'Temperature responses of photosynthesis and respiration in a sub-Antarctic megaherb from Heard Island', *Functional Plant Biology*, vol. 42, 2015, pp. 552–564, doi.org/10.1071/FP14134, accessed 3 May 2022.

FOR SPECIFIC SPECIES

Acaena anserinifolia
Thorsen, MJ, PJ Seddon and KJM Dickinson, 'Faunal influences on New Zealand seed dispersal characteristics', *Evolutionary Ecology*, vol. 25, no. 6, 2011, pp. 1397–1426.

Arthropodium cirratum
Shepherd, LD, M Bulgarella and PJ de Lange, 'Genetic structuring of the coastal herb *Arthropodium cirratum* (Asparagaceae) is shaped by low gene flow, hybridization and prehistoric translocation', *PLoS One*, vol. 13, no. 10, 2018, e0204943, doi.org/10.1371/journal.pone.0204943, accessed 3 May 2022.

Asplenium flabellifolium
Brownsey, PJ and LR Perrie, 'Aspleniaceae', in: Breitwieser, I and AD Wilton, *Flora of New Zealand – Ferns and Lycophytes*, Fascicle 18, Manaaki Whenua Press, Lincoln, 2018, dx.doi.org/10.7931/B1562D, accessed 3 May 2022.

Clematis forsteri
Heenan, PB and J Cartman, 'Reinstatement of *Clematis petriei* (Ranunculaceae), and typification and variation of *C. forsteri*', *New Zealand Journal of Botany*, vol. 38, no. 4, 2000, pp. 575–585, doi.org/10.1080/002882 5X.2000.9512706, accessed 3 May 2022.

Coprosma lucida
Crawford, JC, 'On New Zealand coffee', *Transactions of the New Zealand Institute*, vol. 9, 1877, pp. 545–546, biodiversitylibrary.org/item/104345#page/588/mode/1up, accessed 3 May 2022.

Didymocheton spectabilis
Holzmeyer, L, F Hauenschild, DJ Mabberley and AN Muellner-Riehl, 'Confirmed polyphyly, generic recircumscription and typification of *Dysoxylum* (Meliaceae), with revised disposition of currently accepted species', *Taxon*, vol. 70, no. 6, 2021, pp. 1248–1272, doi.org/10.1002/tax.12591, accessed 3 May 2022.

Entelea arborescens
Shepherd, LD, J Frericks, PJ Biggs and PJ de Lange, 'Phylogeography of the endemic New Zealand tree *Entelea arborescens* (whau; Malvaceae)', *New Zealand Journal of Botany*, vol. 57, no. 3, 2019, pp. 154–168, doi.org/10.1080/00 28825X.2019.1577277, accessed 3 May 2022.

Gaultheria antipoda
Morgan-Richards, M, S Trewick and S Dunavan, 'When is it coevolution? The case of ground wētā and fleshy fruits in New Zealand', *New Zealand Journal of Ecology*, vol. 32, 2008, pp. 108–112, newzealandecology.org/nzje/2843, accessed 3 May 2022.

Whitaker, AH, 'The roles of lizards in New Zealand plant reproductive strategies', *New Zealand Journal of Botany*, vol. 25, no. 2, 1987, pp. 315–328, doi.org/10.1080/0028825X.1987.10410078, accessed 3 May 2022.

Young, LM, D Kelly and XJ Nelson, 'Alpine flora may depend on declining frugivorous parrot for seed dispersal', *Biological Conservation*, vol. 147, no. 1, 2012, pp. 133–142, doi.org/10.1016/j.biocon.2011.12.023, accessed 3 May 2022.

Griselinia lucida
Bryan, CL, BD Clarkson and MJ Clearwater, 'Biological flora of New Zealand 12: *Griselinia lucida*, puka, akapuka, akakōpuka, shining broadleaf', *New Zealand Journal of Botany*, vol. 49, no. 4, 2011, pp. 461–479, doi.org/10.1080/0 028825X.2011.603342, accessed 3 May 2022.

Lepidium oleraceum
de Lange, PJ, PB Heenan, JR Rolfe, GJ Houliston and AD Mitchell, 'New *Lepidium* (Brassicaceae) from New Zealand', *PhytoKeys*, no. 24, 2013, pp. 1–147, doi.org/10.3897/phytokeys.24.4375, accessed 3 May 2022.

Lophomyrtus bullata
Beresford, R, G Smith, B Ganley and R Campbell, 'Impacts of myrtle rust in New Zealand since its arrival in 2017', *New Zealand Garden Journal*, vol. 22, no. 2, 2019, pp. 5–10, myrtlerust.org.nz/assets/news/NZ-Garden-Journal-Dec-2019-p5-10.pdf, accessed 3 May 2022.

Ho, WH, J Baskarathevan, RL Griffin, BD Quinn, BJ Alexander, D Havell, N Ward and A Pathan, 'First report of myrtle rust caused by *Austropuccinia psidii* on *Metrosideros kermadecensis* on Raoul Island and on *M. excelsa* in Kerikeri, New Zealand', *Plant Disease,* vol. 103, no. 8, 2019, p. 2128, apsjournals.apsnet.org/doi/10.1094/PDIS-12-18-2243-PDN, accessed 3 May 2022.

Metrosideros excelsa
Bylsma, RJ, BD Clarkson and JT Efford, 'Biological flora of New Zealand 14: *Metrosideros excelsa*, pōhutukawa, New Zealand Christmas tree', *New Zealand Journal of Botany*, vol. 52, no. 3, 2014, pp. 365–385, doi.org/10.1080/002882 5X.2014.926278, accessed 3 May 2022.

Nertera depressa
Wood, JR, SJ Richardson, MS McGlone and JM Wilmshurst, 'The diets of moa (Aves: Dinornithiformes)', *New Zealand Journal of Ecology*, vol. 44, no. 1, 2020, pp. 1–21, jstor.org/stable/26872856, accessed 3 May 2022.

Passiflora tetrandra
Krosnick, SE, AJ Ford, and JV Freudenstein, 'Taxonomic revision of *Passiflora* subgenus *Tetrapathea* including the monotypic genera *Hollrungia* and *Tetrapathea* (Passifloraceae), and a new species of *Passiflora*', *Systematic Botany*, vol. 34, no. 2, 2009, pp. 375–385, doi. org/10.1600/036364409788606343, accessed 3 May 2022.

Pimelea prostrata
Burrows, CJ, 'Genus *Pimelea* (Thymelaeaceae) in New Zealand 2. The endemic *Pimelea prostrata* and *Pimelea urvilliana* species complexes', *New Zealand Journal of Botany*, vol. 47, no. 2, 2009, pp. 163–229, doi. org/10.1080/00288250909509804, accessed 3 May 2022.

Plantago raoulii
Meudt, HM, 'A taxonomic revision of native New Zealand *Plantago* (Plantaginaceae)', *New Zealand Journal of Botany*, vol. 50, no. 2, 2012, pp. 101–178, doi.org/10.1080/0028825X.2012.671179, accessed 3 May 2022.

Pterophylla racemosa
Pillon, Y, HCF Hopkins, O Maurin, N Epitawalage, J Bradford, ZS Rogers, WJ Baker and F Forest, 'Phylogenomics and biogeography of Cunoniaceae (Oxalidales) with complete generic sampling and taxonomic realignments', *American Journal of Botany*, vol. 108, no. 7, 2021, pp. 1181–1200, doi. org/10.1002/ajb2.1688, accessed 3 May 2022.

Tetragonia tetragonoides
Roskruge, N, The commercialisation of kōkihi or New Zealand spinach (*Tetragonia tetragonioides*) in New Zealand', *Agronomy New Zealand*, vol. 41, 2011, pp. 149–156, cabi.org/isc/FullTextPDF/2012/20123140856.pdf, accessed 3 May 2022.

Veronica salicifolia
Bayly, MJ and A Kellow, *An Illustrated Guide to New Zealand Hebes*, Te Papa Press, New Zealand, 2006.

IMAGE CREDITS

All engravings held by the Museum of New Zealand Te Papa Tongarewa, gift of the British Museum, 1895. They are all based on field sketches by Sydney Parkinson (1745–1771). Parkinson's unfinished sketches were completed by five artists, and copperplate engravings made by a team of eighteen engravers, all under the direction of Joseph Banks.

Page 16: Gerald Sibelius after Sydney Parkinson (1769–1770) and John Frederick Miller.

Pages 18, 82, 88, 94: Gabriel Smith after Sydney Parkinson (1769–1770).

Pages 20, 26, 36, 60, 62, 64, 98, 114: Daniel MacKenzie after Sydney Parkinson (1769–1770).

Pages 22, 66, 76: Gabriel Smith after Sydney Parkinson (1769–1770) and John Frederick Miller.

Pages 24, 44, 46, 50, 52, 54, 56, 58, 68, 70, 74, 80, 84, 90, 104, 110: Gerald Sibelius after Sydney Parkinson (1769–1770) and Frederick Polydore Nodder.

Pages 28, 86, 112: Gerald Sibelius after Sydney Parkinson (1769–1770).

Pages 30, 32, 34, 72, 78, 100: Daniel MacKenzie after Sydney Parkinson (1769–1770) and Frederick Polydore Nodder.

Pages 38, 40: William Tringham after Sydney Parkinson (1769–1770).

Page 42: Bannerman after Sydney Parkinson (1769).

Pages 48, 96: Thomas Scratchley after Sydney Parkinson (1769–1770).

Page 92: Frederick Polydore Nodder after Sydney Parkinson (1769–1770) and Frederick Polydore Nodder.

Page 102: Daniel MacKenzie after Sydney Parkinson (1770) and John Cleveley.

Page 106: Daniel MacKenzie after Sydney Parkinson (1769–1770) and John Frederick Miller.

Page 108: William Tringham after Sydney Parkinson (1769–1770) and John Frederick Miller.

ACKNOWLEDGEMENTS

We would like to thank Patrick Brownsey, Research Associate at
Te Papa, for his valuable suggestions for improving the descriptions, and
Rebecca Rice (Curator Historical New Zealand Art) for advising on and
checking our notes about the illustrations.

Many thanks to Tim Denee for the book and series design, Susi Bailey for
the copy edit, and Teresa McIntyre for the proof read.

INDEX OF SPECIES

Bold page numbers refer to species descriptions.

A
Acaena anserinifolia **19**
Aciphylla squarrosa **21**
Adams mistletoe 9
Aristotelia serrata 8, **57**
Arthropodium cirratum **23**
Asplenium flabellifolium **17**
Austropuccinia psidii 85, 89

B
Bamboo orchid **29**
Bead plant **39**
Beilschmiedia tawa 8, **61**
Bidibid **19**
Brachyglottis repanda **59**
Bush lawyer **55**
Bush snowberry **79**
Bushman's friend **59**
Butterfly fern **17**

C
Calystegia sylvatica 49
Calystegia tuguriorum **49**
Celmisia gracilenta 8, **25**
Clematis forsteri 7, **51**
Clematis petriei 51
Clianthus puniceus **63**
Cook's scurvy grass **31**
Coprosma lucida **65**
Corynocarpus laevigatus **67**
Creeping pratia **35**

D
Dacrydium cupressinum 8, **69**
Dactylanthus taylorii 107
Didymocheton spectabilis **71**
Drosera auriculata **27**
Dysoxylum spectabile see
  Didymocheton spectabilis

E
Earina mucronata **29**
Elaeocarpus dentatus **73**
Elaeocarpus dentatus var. obovatus
  73
Entelea arborescens **75**

F
Five finger **101**
Forget-me-not **37**
Forster's clematis 7, **51**
Fuchsia excorticata 8, **77**

G
Gaultheria antipoda **79**
Glasswort **43**
Griselinia lucida **79**

H
Hīnau **73**

K
Kākā beak **63**
kaikōmako 87
Kāmahi 8, **103**
Karaka **67**
Karamū **65**
Kawakawa **97**
Knightia excelsa **83**
Kohekohe **71**
Kōhia 8, **53**
Kōhūhū **99**
Kōkihi **45**
Koromiko **115**
Kōtukutuku 8, **77**
Kōwhai **111**
Kōwhai ngutu-kākā **63**

L
Lepidium oleraceum **31**
Libertia grandiflora **33**
Lobelia angulata **35**
Lophomyrtus bullata **85**

M
Māhoe **87**
Māikuku **47**
Makomako 8, **57**
Māpou **93**
Melicytus ramiflorus **87**
Metrosideros excelsa **89**
Mikoikoi **33**
Mountain daisy 8, **25**
Myoporum laetum **91**
Myosotis forsteri 8, **37**
Myrsine australis **93**
Myrtle rust 85, 89

N
Nau **31**
Necklace fern **17**
Nertera depressa **39**
New Zealand
    bindweed **49**
    christmas tree **89**
    cork tree **75**
    daphne **95**
    gloxinia **105**
    honeysuckle **83**
    iris **33**
    mahogany **71**
    passionflower 8, **53**
    spinach
Ngaio **91**

O
Ongaonga **113**

P
Pānakenake **35**
Passiflora tetrandra 8, **53**
Patē 101, **107**
Peka-a-waka **29**
Pekapeka **25**
Pennantia corymbosa 87
Pepper tree **97**
Pimelea prostrata **95**

Pinātoro **95**
Piper excelsum **97**
Piripiri **19**
Pittosporum tenuifolium **99**
Plantago raoulii **41**
Pōānanga **51**
Pōhutukawa **89**
Poroporo **109**
Pōwhiwhi **49**
Pseudopanax arboreus **101**
Pterophylla racemosa 8, **103**
Pua o te rēinga 107
Puka **79**

R
Ramarama **85**
Rangiora **59**
Rengarenga **23**
Rengarenga lily **23**
Rewarewa **83**
Rhabdothamnus solandri **105**
Rimu 8, **69**
Rubus australis **55**

S
Salicornia quinqueflora **43**
Schefflera digitate **107**
Seven finger 101, **107**
Shining broadleaf **79**
Solanum aviculare **109**
Sophora tetraptera **111**
Speargrass **21**
Sundew **27**

T
Taramea **21**
Tātarāmoa **55**
Taurepo **105**
Tawa 8, **61**
Tāwiniwini **79**
Tetragonia tetragonoides **45**
Thelymitra longifolia **47**
Tree fuchsia 8, **77**
Tree nettle **113**
Trilepidea adamsii 9
Tūkōrehu **41**

U
Ureure **43**
Urtica ferox **113**

V
Veronica salicifolia **115**

W
Walking fern **17**
Weinmannia racemosa see
 Pterophylla racemosa
Whau **75**
Whauwhaupaku **101**
White sun orchid **47**
Wineberry 8, **57**

ABOUT THE AUTHORS

Dr Carlos Lehnebach is a Botany Curator at Te Papa and studies the diversity, evolution and conservation of Aotearoa flowering plants. His main groups of interest are terrestrial and epiphytic orchids, alpine plants and plants shared with other land masses in the southern hemisphere. His current projects aim to describe the New Zealand orchid flora and develop methods to assist the conservation of rare and threatened plants.

Dr Heidi Meudt is a Botany Curator at Te Papa. Her current collections-based research focuses on the evolution and classification of native Aotearoa flowering plants, especially forget-me-nots (*Myosotis*). She uses morphology, pollen, DNA and other data to understand how many species there are, how they can be identified and where they are found. Her research aims to update the taxonomy and conservation status of all native forget-me-nots. She also studies native foxgloves (*Ourisia*), plantains (*Plantago*) and hebes (*Veronica*) throughout the southern hemisphere.

First published in New Zealand in 2022 by
Te Papa Press, PO Box 467, Wellington, New Zealand
www.tepapapress.co.nz

Text: Carlos Lehnebach and Heidi Meudt
© Museum of New Zealand Te Papa Tongarewa
Images: as credited on page 126

This book is copyright. Apart from any fair dealing
for the purpose of private study, research, criticism,
or review, as permitted under the Copyright Act, no part
of this book may be reproduced by any process, stored
in a retrieval system, or transmitted in any form, without
the prior permission of the Museum of New Zealand
Te Papa Tongarewa.

TE PAPA® is the trademark of the Museum of
New Zealand Te Papa Tongarewa
Te Papa Press is an imprint of the Museum of
New Zealand Te Papa Tongarewa

A catalogue record is available from the National Library
of New Zealand

ISBN 978-1-99-115093-6

Cover and internal design by Tim Denee
Cover illustration based on the leaf of the kawakawa
(pepper tree, *Piper excelsum*)

Printed by Everbest Printing Investment Limited